Defiant MK.I Combat Log

Fighter Command

May-September 1940

Hugh Harkins

Defiant MK.I
Combat Log

© Hugh Harkins 2014

Published by Centurion Publishing
United Kingdom
G65 9YE

ISBN 10: 1-903630-47-9
ISBN 13: 978-1-903630-47-1

This volume first published 2014

The Publishers and Author would like to thank all organisations and services for
their assistance and contributions in the preparation of this publication

CONTENTS

INTRODUCTION

The purpose of this volume is to provide a comprehensive detailed study of the operational and combat operations of the RAF's Boulton Paul Defiant MK.I turret armed fighter aircraft during the hectic air battles of mid and late May 1940, the latter period of which the Defiant was heavily involved in operations against Luftwaffe fighters and bombers attacking the British Expeditionary Force evacuation operations on the channel coast, particularly around Dunkirk. It also covers the Defiants operations in the air battles of July and August at the height of the Battle of Britain, when 264 Squadron and 141 Squadron flew day and night operations, suffering severe losses.

A brief description of the genesis and development of the Defiant MK.I fighter is laid down, but the volume is not designed to be a comprehensive monograph on that subject. A brief description of the Defiants main fighter adversary, the German Me.109E, is also provided.

The volume is copiously supported by a wealth of operational documents including Squadron Narratives, Group Intelligence Combat Reports, Squadron operational Records and pilot Personal Combat Reports, many of which are reproduced verbatim. Operational documents have been tied up against German reports whenever possible which naturally results in areas of disputed figures, particularly with regards to numbers of German aircraft shot down.

There are a number of incidences of German He.112 and He.113 fighters being engaged or observed, however, it should be noted that such aircraft were not operational with the Luftwaffe and these sightings, therefore, must be assumed to have been Me.109's, British Spitfire or Hurricane fighters or an even French fighters; the latter being unlikely.

1

BOULTON PAUL DEFIANT MK.I

The Boulton Paul Defiant MK.I was designed primarily as a defensive fighter to be used in standing patrols, day or night, to counter attacks on Great Britain by bomber aircraft. Instead, the Defiant found itself conducting fighter sweeps over the Low Countries and Northern France in May 1940 in attempts to counter the Luftwaffe attacks during the German conquest of North Western Europe. During these sweeps the Defiant met with early success against German bombers and Me.110 and Me.109 fighters; these successes being marred by later heavy losses.

There are many areas which could be selected as the start point for the turret armed fighter; but for the purposes of this volume Air Ministry Specification F.5/33, issued in 1933 for a modern monoplane fighter aircraft armed with a battery of machine guns in a power operated turret has been selected as an acceptable start point. For this, Boulton & Paul put forward their P.76 twin-engine design, competing with designs from Gloster, Bristol (Type 140) and Armstrong Whitworth (A.W. 34). None of these designs was considered suitable and the teams went back to their respective drawing boards.

A new revised Specification, F.9/35, was issued by the Air Ministry on 26 June 1935. The competing manufacturers were called on to design a two-crew fighter equipped with a single power operated four gun turret, which would be the aircrafts sole armament. This concept was a departure from the types it was to replace such as the Hawker Demon bi-plane fighter which featured fixed forward firing and a rear firing gun. A maximum speed of at least 298 mph was required at altitudes of around 15,000 ft; an altitude it was to be capable of reaching in around 5.5 minutes. Required ceiling was put at 33,000 ft.

The Boulton Paul P.82 was eventfully selected, among other designs, to go to the prototype development stage. The aircraft that emerged superficially resembled the Hawker Hurricane single-seat monoplane fighter, being of clean design, particularly before the turret was fitted. On 28 April 1937 the Air Ministry ordered 87 production model P.82's, for which serial numbers L6950-L7036 were issued. Around this time the name Defiant was applied to the new fighter, the prototype of which, K8310, flew on 11 August that year. This flight, conducted from Pendeford Airport by Cecil Feather, was conducted without the turret fitted; a fairing being fitted over the area it was to occupy. Early flight tests produced good performance figures, with speeds of up to 320 mph achieved, albeit without the turret and other items of military equipment installed. It was of course realised that these speeds would not be achieved by service aircraft.

The Defiant MK.I day fighter equipped two Fighter Command Squadrons in 1940. This quartet is from No.264 Squadron on a patrol in summer 1940. RAF

In February 1938 a production order was received for 202 Defiant MK.I fighters, with a further order placed in May that year. That same month the prototype, K8310, was equipped with its MK IID power operated turret, which would carry four x 0.303 in Browning machine guns with 600 rounds carried for each gun. Armament trials with the turret were conducted over the Orfordness (Orford Ness) ranges in February 1938, with the aircraft operating from

Martlesham Heath. In October that year further performance trials with the turret and armament installed revealed a top speed of 303 mph at altitudes of 15-17,000 ft, with 15,000 ft being reached in 10.1 minutes. Some figures were lower than had been anticipated, but were considered acceptable for the aircraft's role. Although the aircraft possessed good handling characteristics it was considerably inferior to the new generation single-seat monoplane fighters entering service in the shape of the Hawker Hurricane MK.I and Supermarine Spitfire MK.I, both of which were also considerably faster and possessed a higher all round performance to the two-crew Defiant. At the time this was not considered to be too much of a handicap as the Defiant was expected to operate against bombers, although it must have been realised that bomber formations may be expected to be escorted by fighters.

The second prototype, K8620, which received modifications, the requirement for which was revealed during flight tests of the first prototype, conducted its maiden flight on 18 May 1938. Although designed to be more or less representative of what the production aircraft would emerge as, it was discovered during flight testing that a new, larger, rudder was required.

The prototype Boulton Paul P.82 (Defiant), K8310, prior to fitment of its turret. The aircraft conducted its maiden flight, without the turret fitted, on 11 August 1937. MAP

The prototype Defiant, K8310, equipped with its turret, which was fitted in February 1938. MAP

The first flight of a production Defiant MK.I, Serial L6950, was conducted on 30 July 1939, by which time war clouds were gathering over the horizon on the European Continent. Only 3 production Defiants had been delivered by the time Britain and France declared war on Germany on 3 September 1939, and by the end of the month this figure had increased only to five.

During the period of the Battle of Britain the use of the Defiant leaned more towards its original concept, but by this time the aircraft was more understood by the Luftwaffe. While its capability against the Me.109E is still hotly debated more than 70 years after the air battles of 1940, it should be concluded that a well flown Me.109 was far more likely to emerge victorious against a well flown Defiant when neither aircraft had a definite tactical advantage. This hypothesis is the one reached by trials conducted against captured Me.109's and the one subscribed to by the RAF and Air Ministry of the time.

During the early engagements between the two types in mid-May 1940 the Defiant was often mistaken for the Hawker Hurricane; a type with which it had a superficial resemblance. Me.109 pilots attacking from astern, abeam or above could be caught unawares when suddenly they flew into a hail of .303 bullets from the Defiants turret. However, as the campaign progressed the Defiants strengths and weakness were more appreciated by Luftwaffe fighter pilots who devised tactics accordingly.

It is often stated that the Defiant could easily hold its own against the Me.109E by adopting a so called 'Descending Defensive Circle', whereby the Defiants decreased altitude gradually while flying in the defensive circle. This was apparently designed to prevent Me.109E's from attacking from underneath. However, this tactic, although often lauded as being standard, was never really used in the hectic air battles of 1940. In truth, such a tactic was tactically impracticable for a defensive fighter which was tasked with intercepting enemy bombers, during which it could itself be intercepted by enemy fighters. The defensive circle would also be far too vulnerable as it removed any real scope for the Defiant pilots to take evasive action. Like bombers forming defensive formations, Defiants could no doubt shoot down enemy fighters using this method, but in all probability at too high a cost in losses to their own formation.

In fighter vs. fighter mock combats flown with Defiants L6951 and L6952 against Hurricane MK.I's in early 1940, the Defiant came off second best. It was clear from this early stage that the Defiant was no march for modern single-seat, single-engine monoplane fighters designed for combat with other fighters. Trials against a No.65 Squadron Supermarine Spitfire I in early April 1940 again showed the fixed gun single-seat fighter to be superior. Mock attacks conducted against a Bristol Blenheim IV twin-engine bomber were more satisfactory, although when attacking from underneath it was found that the Blenheim could outpace the Defiant by entering a steep dive.

It is fair to conclude that when Me.109E's encountered Defiants, recognising them as such, the Defiants would more often than not suffer high loss, as borne out by actual operations. The conclusions drawn by the powers that be at the time were that while the theory of the turret fighter, which in essence saw the pilot position his aircraft with the air gunners field of fire as a main priority, was sound against slow flying bomber formations, but was considered difficult if not impossible against high speed maneuverable fighters, whereby the fight could degenerate into a dogfight. This fact more than any other would see the Defiant move completely to the Night Fighter role in September 1940, a month in which only a few emergency defensive scrambles and convoy protection patrols were flown in daylight hours. Over the next few years the Defiant grew into a competent Night Fighter, Squadrons eventually receiving the more capable Defiant MK. II.

2

264 SQUADRON FORMATION AND EARLY OPERATIONS

No.264 (Madras Presidency) Squadron was originally formed in August 1918 at Suda Bay Crete, where one Flight, No.439, was based, with a second Flight, No.440, based at Syra. Equipped with Seaplanes the squadron had a less than eventful war, flying anti-submarine patrols over the shipping lines of communications for the Allied Forces on the Salonika Front and Aegean Islands for the last few months of the war which ended on 11 November 1918, the Squadron disbanding on 1 March the following year.

No.264 Squadron reformed at RAF Sutton Bridge on 30 October 1939, just less than two months after Britain and France had declared war on Germany on 3 September that year. Over the next 2 weeks personnel were assembled and on 14 November Fighter Command notified the squadron that it was to be equipped with the Boulton Paul Defiant MK.I turret fighter. This was confirmed to Squadron personnel by the Commander in Chief. On the 21st, Fighter Command issued orders for the squadron to move to Martlesham Heath. The CO (Commanding Officer), S/Ldr. Hardy, went to Northolt on the 25th, to fly in a Defiant with the AFDU (Air Fighting Development Unit). P/O's Toyne and Stokes flew a Defiant at the AFDU on the 27th, returning to Northolt the following day. On the 28th, two more No.264 Squadron pilots, P/O's Young and Temple, flew in a Defiant at the AFDU. Before the month was out S/Ldr. Hardy had again flown in a Defiant as the squadron built up experience prior to receiving its own Defiant aircraft. On 2 December, F/Sgt. Richardson and Sgt. Kempster went to the Boulton Paul facility at Wolverhampton for a 4 day course, which commenced on the 4th, on which date an advance party from 264 Squadron began the move to Martlesham Heath, followed by the main party, which departed Sutton Bridge on the 7th.

The sole armament of the Defiant was the quad mounting of 0.303 in machine guns housed in the power operated turret located behind the cockpit. RAF

The Squadron began receiving Defiant MK.I aircraft when F/Lt. Cooke and P/O. Stokes were dispatched to RAF Brize Norton on 8 December 1939 to collect 2 Defiants (some sources claim three Defiants were delivered on this date, but Squadron records show only two aircraft being collected). The Squadron continued to train on Fairey Battle light bomber aircraft, one of which crashed while being ferried from Rissington to Martlesham Heath on 16 December, the pilot, P/O Tipple, unfortunately being killed. By 20 December all Squadron pilots had flown solo on the Battle and the following day two more Defiants were collected from Hullavington by F/Lt. Toyne and P/O. Stokes.

On 11 January 1940 practice attacks with Defiants were conducted and speed trials on the Defiant were conducted on the 24th. By the 25th, pilots were reporting increasing instances of undercarriage "Oleo" legs apparently dropping down during flight.

On 26 January a No.1 practice attack in a Defiant was conducted with a camera gun functioning for post flight analysis. On this date F/Lt. Cooke experienced an engine failure in a Defiant; the same pilot had experienced engine failures in two separate Defiants the previous day. These failures resulted in the grounding of all Defiant aircraft from 28 January, on which date personnel from Rolls Royce arrived to investigate the causes.

The grounding lifted, a pilot was sent to Shawbury on 2 February to collect a Defiant, while another pilot was sent to St Athan on the 4th to collect another

Defiant. However, both pilots returned to Martlesham Heath on the 6th and 7th respectively without their Defiant aircraft as weather conditions were "unsuitable".

On 11 February "relative speed tests with a Hurricane aircraft on No.56 Squadron" were conducted, and on the 15th a Defiant was flown on a night test flight to check out the aircraft and equipment for use at night.

Two more Defiants were collected from Shawbury on 16 February, one of which, flown by P/O. Thomas, force landed at Clapton, but was undamaged.

On 24 February HQ (Headquarters) Fighter Command issued orders for one section from 264 Squadron to go to RAF Northolt on 4 March for "affiliation to Wellingtons". On the 29th a series of test flights to evaluate the Defiants potential as a dive bomber were conducted, with eight bombs released over the range at Orfordness

March started with the loss of Defiant L6962 on the 1st. The aircraft suffered an engine failure and force landed, with its undercarriage up, about a half a mile from Martlesham Heath. On this date Defiant L6951 was flown to the Boulton Paul factory at Wolverhampton for a 30 hour inspection. On the 3rd, Defiant L6974 was collected from RAF St Athan.

In line with the order issued on 24 February, 5 Defiants led by S/Ldr. Hardy were flown to Northolt for trails with the AFDU. Another Defiant, L6975, was delivered to the Squadron after collection from St Athan and two more Defiants were collected from Hullavington on the 11th.

On 20 March a signal was sent to Group stating that two sections of No.264 Squadron "were ready for operational duties". The following day two sections, each of three Defiants, were ordered to go to RAF Wittering "for Operational Duties", arriving there on the 22nd, on which date the squadron's first operational sorties were flown; 4 Defiants flown by F/Lt. Cooke, P/O Kay, P/O Whitley and P/O Stokes, flying convoy protection patrols.

On 24 March, S/Ldr. Hunter assumed command of No.264 Squadron; S/Ldr. Hardy having been promoted to acting Wing Commander effective from 1 March 1940.

On 1 April S/Ldr. Hunter took 'B' Flight detachment to the AFDU at Northolt, returning on the 5th. On the 1st Defiant L6970 was collected from 27 MU (Maintenance Unit) at Shawbury and two more were collected from St Athan on the 5th, on which date a Defiant flown by S/Ldr Hunter and a Spitfire I from No.65 Squadron were flown in a test of "Fixed-v-Free gun fighter".

The Squadron lost another Defiant on 23 April when the aircraft crashed after it caught fire in flight near Orfordness. On 4 May Defiant L6972 force landed after suffering a burst hydraulic pressure gauge. The aircraft suffered only minor damage and none of the crew was injured. From the previous day, 3 May, No.264 Squadron was tasked to have one Defiant "maintained at readiness from dusk preparedness to dawn preparedness". The role was to intercept any intruder aircraft during the hours of darkness

3

264 SQUADRON OPERATIONS OVER THE LOW COUNTRIES AND FRANCE – 10-31 MAY 1940

As the anticipated German Blitzkrieg against the Low Countries and France commenced in the early morning of 10 May 1940 the Allied Armies massed on the Franco-Belgian border put into operation Plan 'D' (Dyle); the move into Belgium to meet the German advance as the Germans were punching deep into Holland through ground and airborne operations. In line with previous doctrine the British Air Forces in France were reinforced by four Hurricane Squadrons, bringing to ten the number of such Squadrons operating in France.

The Dutch had some initial success in frustrating German airborne assaults against such centers as the Hague, but these would be temporary in nature as the German attack had secured many vital objectives, including airfields, which included Ypenburg aerodrome near the Hague. The Dutch accordingly requested British assistance, including the requirement for the RAF to operate over Holland. Ground attack operations were flown by Blenheim MK.IF twin-engine fighters of 600 Squadron Fighter Command on the 10th, followed by a later Blenheim Bombers; the Blenheim fighters suffering heavily, with five out of a formation of six that had attacked Waalhaven being shot down by German Me-110 twin-engine fighters. Over the next few days Fighter Command Spitfires, Hurricanes and the Defiants of 264 Squadron flew many sorties over Holland, particularly over The Hague, but the inexorable tide of the German advance was such that little could be done to slow it, let alone stop it, and Holland accordingly surrendered on 15 May.

10 May 1940: Operational sorties commenced when a single Defiant flown by F/Lt. Skelton with P/O Hatfield as AG (Air Gunner) took off at 01.00 hours for a night air defence sortie. No enemy aircraft were encountered and the aircraft landed back at Martlesham about an hour after take-off. There appears to be no mention of this sortie in the Squadron Form 541, although it is listed in other records including the Form 540.

A few hours after this sortie the hammer fell on the Allied Forces in France and the Low Countries as the German Blitzkrieg commenced. No.264 Squadron was ordered to move to RAF Duxford, where it arrived later in the day and was declared ready for operations by 18.00 hours.

11 May 1940: No.264 Squadron was ordered to have one section of Defiants at "readiness" from 04.30 hours. The only operational sorties were a convoy escort by two Defiants from Red Section, flown by S/Ldr. Hunter & P/O Young. This convoy escort patrol was conducted in the area of the Happisburgh Lightship off the Norfolk Coast, with the Defiants not landing at Duxford until after sunset.

12 May 1940: No.264 Squadron flew its first operational sorties over the continent when 'A' Flight was ordered to patrol near The Hague in company with six Spitfires, Blue and Green Sections of No.66 Squadron. The following 264 Squadron narrative details the operation. The Narrative is reproduced verbatim:

"'A' Flight proceeded to Horsham St. Faith where they refueled and linked up with six Spitfires of 'B' Flight, 66 Squadron, flying direct to the Dutch Coast to patrol near the Hague. Red Section consisted of S/L. Hunter & L.A.C. King (Red 1), P/O Whitehouse & Sgt. Smalley (2), and P/O Young & L.A.C. Johnson (3). Yellow Section being composed of F/Lt. Cooke & Cpl. Lippett (Yellow 1) P/O. Barwell & Sgt. Quinnie (2), (Yellow 3 (P/O Whitley & L.A.C. Turner) returning just after take off). The Flight took off from Horsham at 13.10 hours, commencing patrol at The Hague at 13.55 hours, each section behind a Spitfire Section. An aircraft afterwards identified as a Ju.88, was seen approaching and dropped one bomb near three destroyers at 14.10 hours. Red Section cut him off as he turned to port (inland) and dived almost to ground level. An overtaking attack was commenced then each machine made a 'cross-over' attack in turn. Tracer bullets could be seen entering the Junkers, smoke poured from its port engine and it crashed in the middle of a field which was full of cows and surrounded by dykes. Meanwhile Yellow Section with a section of Spitfires had sighted a Heinkel 111 at 3,000 ft., which promptly dived to ground level. Whilst three Spitfires attacked from behind, Yellow 1 carried out a 'cross-over' attack, from the starboard side, when smoke immediately issued from both engines. Yellow 2 was in a position to make a 'cross-over' attack from the port side when the machine crashed in a field, ending up against a hedge. After delivering

their respective attacks and no other enemy aircraft being observed near at hand, each section returned to Duxford safely, Red Section landing at 15.25 hours and Yellow Section at 15.35 hours. There were no injuries sustained be (should probably read 'by') any personnel or aircraft".

The following account of the patrol, reproduced verbatim, comes from S/Ldr. Leigh, Blue Section Leader of No.66 Squadron:

"Blue and Green sections of No.66 Squadron took off from Horsham for the Hague at 1320 hours. We arrived at The Hague at 1400 hours, at about 7000 feet. We were accompanied by 2 sections of 264 Squadron (Defiants). At about 1415 hours Green Section sighted a Heinkel 111 or Ju.88 which had just bombed three destroyers. I first saw the enemy A/C going inland losing height until it was extremely low. Green section and one Blue A/C and at least one Defiant carried out attacks and eventually smoke was seen coming from the E/A and it touched the ground at about 180 m.p.h. Visibility at the time was good, there was a thin layer of cloud at 8000 ft. Blue and Green Sections continued to patrol up and down the coast, but I personally saw no other E/A. At about 1430 hours I ordered Blue and Green Sections to return home.
Blue Section eventually hit the coast near Norwich and landed at Duxford at 1530 hours."

R.HA. Leigh.   S/Ldr.
Blue Leader. 66 Squadron

The Ju.88 that was attacked after bombing the Destroyers was claimed by 264 Squadron and no less than three Spitfire pilots from No.66 Squadron.

No.264 Squadron Aircraft and Crews involved in the above operation were as follows

Aircraft	Pilot	AG	Take off time	Land time
L6973	S/Ldr. Hunter	LAC King	13.10	15.25
L6972	P/O Whitehouse	Sgt. Smalley	13.10	15.35
L7003	P/O Young	LAC Johnson	13.10	15.25
L6964	P/O Barwell	Sgt. Quinnie	13.10	15.25
L6975	F/Lt. Cooke	Cpl. Lippett	13.10	15.35
L6970	P/O Whitley	LAC Turner	13.10	14.00

No.66 Squadron Spitfires involved in the patrol were as follows:

Aircraft (Spitfire I)	Take off time	Land time
N3182	13.15	15.30
N3042	13.15	15.30
N3043	13.15	15.30
N3044	13.15	15.30
N3121	13.15	15.30

Note: Six Spitfires were involved in the patrol, but only the five noted above were listed in the Squadrons Form 541

Later in the day it was arranged for No.264 Squadrons 'B' Flight, Blue and Green Sections, to go to Martlesham Heath, for where they departed at 19.00 hours to prepare to go on patrol – flown early the following morning.

13 May 1940: Six Defiants from 'B' Flight, L6969 (F/Lt. Skelton/P/O Hatfield), L6960 (P/O Chandler/LAC McLeish), L6958 (P/O Thomas/LAC Bromley), L6977 (P/O Greenhouse/Sgt. Greenhalgh), L6965 (P/O McLeod/LAC Cox) and L6974 (P/O Kay/LAC Jones), that had flown to Martlesham Heath the previous evening, took off at 04.15 hours to patrol The Hague.

The following is taken verbatim from the Squadron Narrative of the operation:

"... took off from Martlesham Heath at 0430 hours on 13/5/40, each section following a section of Spitfires of 'A' Flight 66 Squadron. Their objective was to attack enemy troop transports along the Dutch coast north of The Hague. The coast was struck about ten miles north of The Hague at 0515 hours when all a/c proceeded north. When over IUMUIDEN (should probably read Ijmuiden) **intense Dutch A.A. gun fire was encountered which caused the sections to turn about. More A.A. fire, this time German, was met over MAASSLUIS, which caused sections to take evasive action. Shortly afterwards the Spitfires turned sharply inland, diving from 6,000 feet as a number of a/c were spotted, and the Defiants followed.**
The flight attacked a number of Ju.87's and were themselves attacked by Me.109's and all, with the exception of P.O. Kay and L.A.C. Jones, were shot down.
F/Lt. Skelton was killed but his gunner P.O. Hatfield baled out and P.O. Thomas also baled out after his gunner, L.A.C. Bromely had been killed.

P.O. Hatfield saw a Defiant explode in the air and this I presumed to be the aircraft flown by P.O. Chandler with L.A.C. McLeish. P.O. Kay landed at KNOCKE, refueled and then returned. Four Ju.87's and one Me.109 were brought down".

During the above operation Defiants L6969, L6960, L6958, L6977 and L6965 were shot down, while L6964 returned to base at 06.30.

The following day P/O Thomas and P/O Hatfield arrived back at base from Holland. After being shot down they met at Sleewyk in Holland where they were apparently arrested and almost shot out of hand as German Spies. It appears that their "Dutch Captor" was a fifth columnist. On their return, P/O Hatfield reported that while descending in his parachute he was fired at from the ground, presumably by the Dutch. After being shot down "at ZEUENBERGEN, HOLLAND" they had apparently donned civilian clothes to escape capture by the Germans who were in possession of Zeuenbergen.

On the 17th, P/O McLeod and LAC Cox returned, having embarked on a Destroyer at Antwerp, which then landed them at Folkestone.

Following the operations of the 12th and 13th a Telegram received from Messrs. Boulton Paul Aircraft Ltd, read: - "Squadron Leader Hunter and squadron. Congratulations on first blood..." On the 15th the Officer Commanding No.12 Group sent the following message to 264 Squadron: "I want to congratulate No.264 Squadron most heartily on the success of their operations over Holland which have proved the success of the Defiant as a fighter. I much regret the loss that 'B' Flight suffered in the second operation. (Signed) T. Leigh Mallory A.V.M. Commanding No.12 Group". Propaganda or sticking their collective heads in the sand; it should have been clear to 12 Group that the Defiant was coming up wanting when it encountered determined enemy fighter opposition. It is interesting to note that 66(Spitfire) Squadron claimed 3 confirmed 3 possible and one doubtful from the battle for the British claim of 4 Ju.87 and 1 Me.109's destroyed.

Following the severe losses of the 13th, 264 Squadron was stood down from operations over the continent where events on the ground were moving very fast. Air Chief Marshal Dowding, the Commander in Chief of Fighter Command, whom had been campaigning against the sending of large numbers of British fighter aircraft to France, appeared before the War Cabinet on the 15th. He successfully pleaded his case that the fighters should be retained in Britain, although smaller numbers of Hawker Hurricanes would later be sent to France; operating over France, but returning to Southern England after operational sorties.

As the northern group of Allied Armies retreated in the face of the German Panzer formations, it had become clear that the unthinkable would have to be thought about. The evacuation of the BEF (British Expeditionary Force) from France was no longer considered a possibility, but by the of 19th May, the same day that Lord Gort, the Commander in Chief of the BEF, was ordered to fight his way south, evacuation seemed a distinct possibility; the strategic situation being much more ominous that it had been only a day or so before. Even this early in the campaign it had become clear to the British High Command that with the resources at hand the Germans were unlikely to be stopped. The best that could be hoped for was a temporary setback.

Over the next seven days the Allied Armies in the North were forced back into an ever shrinking defensive perimeter around the strategic channel ports. It was now clear that the BEF would have to be either evacuated to Britain or be lost. To accept that latter was unthinkable if Britain was to continue the fight, as the loss of its field Army would increase the pressure on the already hard pressed French. Without a field Army the fall of France would inevitably mean the defeat of Britain, which would either have to ask the Germans for terms or fight on and be defeated. It was clear that Britain had every intention of fighting on, even in the event of a French collapse. Therefore, it was decided that the BEF had to be evacuated at all costs.

Operation Dynamo officially commenced when Admiral Ramsey issued the order for the evacuation of the BEF at 18.57 hours on 26 May 1940. The Channel port of Boulogne had been evacuated on 23/24 May and Calais was overrun after the garrison was ordered to fight to the end; its brave defenders being smashed by overwhelming force as the Germans tightened their stranglehold on the Dunkirk pocket.

The vessel *Shikari* was the last to leave Dunkirk at 03.40 am on the morning of 4 June; this vessel being ineffectively bombed en route to England. Admiralty message 1423/4 officially terminated Operation Dynamo at 11.00 hours on Tuesday 4 June 1940, by which time more than a third of a million British and Allied troops had been evacuated, and this fact more than any other meant that Britain could continue the fight, not only on the Home Front and Northern European Theatre, but also in the Mediterranean, which would soon be in dire need of reinforcements.

Despite the high level attempts to have Fighter Command all but sit out the critical battle raging on the continent, the situation was so dire for the Allied Armies being cut off in the North of France and Belgium and awaiting evacuation that Fighter Command was ordered at the highest levels of Government to commit some of its Squadrons to the battle that was so crucial to the survival of Britain. While Dowding saw the critical battle as that which he considered was still to be fought over Britain, others, perhaps looking more at the bigger picture, realised that the survival of at least a significant portion of the BEF was the real life blood of the nation, that if severed, would surely lead to Britain's defeat should France Fall. It was realised at the highest levels that having Fighter Command intact following a French capitulation would have been no guarantee of a successful defense against a German invasion, for without an effective army to face an invasion force, a mere handful of German

Divisions being landed, even against a largely intact Fighter Command, would have in all probability met with enormous success very quickly as the military cupboard was essentially bare in the United Kingdom in early late May 1940.

This led to the decision that the evacuation from Dunkirk and surrounding areas had to be protected, despite any protestations by Dowding against Fighter Commands use. The limited range of British single-engine day Fighters; Supermarine Spitfire MK.I, Hawker Hurricane MK.I and Boulton Paul Defiant MK.I, meant that they could not in any case have influenced the wider Battle for France much by operating from Southern England. However, range was adequate to fly patrols over the Dunkirk-Boulogne-Calais area, which would furnish some protection for the hard pressed BEF being evacuated, and the hard pressed Navy and civilian craft conducting the evacuation.

From 22 May, Fighter Command flew in the region of 200 sorties per day over the evacuation areas. However, this number was far too small as the Command successfully held back the vast majority of Squadrons from operations; a mere handful of Fighter Commands available Squadrons being employed at any one time, with a peak of 16 or so Squadrons and 200 aircraft being kept available out of the Commands more than 600 available serviceable aircraft. While the official History records that the whole resources of Fighter Command were being sucked into the battle, nothing could actually have been further from the truth. Dowding was successfully husbanding his resources at the expense of the BEF and Royal Navy, the latter suffering large numbers of valuable Destroyers sunk or damaged. On 1 June for instance, 3 British Destroyers were sunk and 4 damaged. Of the 41 British Destroyers committed to the operation from 26 May until 4 June, 6 were sunk and 23 damaged. Of course, enemy bombing was not the only cause of shipping losses, torpedoes and mines also taking their toll.

With the limited number of Squadrons committed to the operation Air Vice-Marshal Keith Park, Officer Commanding 11 Group, had a difficult job providing protection to the evacuation areas and sea routes during daylight hours. Initially he was putting two Squadrons over the evacuation areas at the same time for most of the daylight hours. This, of course, was much too little to seriously dissuade the Luftwaffe despite the gallant attempts of the aircrew.

A signal from Chief of the Air Staff ,Air Chief Marshal Sir Cyril Newall to the Chiefs of Fighter, Bomber and Coastal Commands on the morning of 28 May read "Today is likely to be the most critical day ever experienced by the British Army. The extreme gravity of the situation should be explained to all units. I am confident that all ranks will appreciate that it is the duty of the R.A.F. to make their greatest effort today to assist their comrades of both the Army and the Navy." The orders for Fighter Command for that day were to "ensure the protection of Dunkirk beaches (three miles on either side) from first light until darkness by continuous fighter patrols in strength", the order continued that the Command was to have "due regard to the protection of bomber sorties and the provision of support of the B.E.F. area". Coastal Command was also heavily involved in the protection of the evacuation, flying more or less continuous daylight patrols between North Goodwins, Kent to Gravelines, 15 miles southwest of Dunkirk, then along the coast to Ostend, Belgium. For this effort it utilised Bristol Blenheim and Lockheed Hudson twin-engine bombers. The FAA (Fleet Air Arm) supported this operation with Blackburn Skua dive bombers and Blackburn Roc turret fighters, formations of up to three aircraft flying at a time.

During the course of 28 May Fighter Command flew a peak of 321 sorties over the evacuation areas and by the time the evacuation ended on the morning of 4 June 1940 the RAF had flown 2,739 fighter, 651 bomber and 171 reconnaissance sorties in support of Operation Dynamo. To this could be added the smaller number of sorties flown by the Fleet Air Arm to protect the sea routes taken by the evacuation vessels. Blackburn Skua dive bombers of 801 and 806 Squadrons FAA were also used to attack German armoured and infantry formations closing on Dunkirk, and German E-Boats operating against the evacuation shipping.

It is certainly no exaggeration that the RAF was very poorly thought off by the soldiers and sailors in the hell that was Dunkirk. While criticism of the high command was, perhaps, warranted, criticism of the pilots and aircrew themselves was unfortunate, although understandable, form men whom were being pounded almost at will by the Luftwaffe.

Admiral Ramsey's report to the Admiralty stated that the RAF was putting its effort in at the wrong places and at the wrong times, with inadequate force. The Admiral wrote "… full air protection was expected, but instead, for hours on end the ships off-shore were subjected to a murderous hail of bombs and machine-gun bullets…" To this was added many reports containing praise for the efforts of the individual pilots and aircrews committed to the operation, but scathing disappointment as to the puny effort afforded by Fighter Command at the height of the operation. Later Admiral Ramsey would submit a more glowing report, no doubt motivated to ensure harmony between the services.

Air Vice-Marshal Park painted a somewhat different picture to Dowding, giving the impression of complete British air superiority over the evacuation areas. Dowding, for his part, was only prepared to allow an average of 200 serviceable fighters to operate over Dunkirk. This figure was of course much too small, meaning Park could not be expected to attain or maintain any real degree of air superiority over the evacuation areas, and despite some local success when fighters were in the right place at the right time, the Luftwaffe was rarely seriously hampered in its operations against the Dunkirk pocket.

In the early part of the operation concentrations of around two Squadrons of RAF fighters at a time were operating over the evacuation areas for much of the daylight hours. In the latter stages of the operation concentrations of up to four Squadrons were flown over the protected areas, but, as no more single-seat fighters were made available, this was achieved at the reduction of the amount of daylight hours that RAF fighters would be over the evacuation areas.

Dowding's unwillingness to make available more than an average of 200 fighters stemmed from his fear that if he provided more fighters it would result in higher losses, reducing his ability to build up his fighter force for the coming air battle over Britain. Others in official circles, supported by Official documentation, considered that, to quote the Official History "It is however possible – if not probable – to contend that a bigger concentration over Dunkirk might have resulted not, as Dowding feared, in higher losses, but in lower." This statement was preceded by the statement that "He could, however, have achieved a larger initial concentration over Dunkirk…"

Other than the fighters of Fighter Command the troops at Dunkirk had only handfuls of shore based anti-aircraft guns and the ship based guns to try and ward off Luftwaffe attacks. Official claims for enemy aircraft destroyed by ships gunfire off Dunkirk from 27 May to 1 June was 35, with 21 others claimed damaged. Of course, like the claims made by the fighters of Fighter Command, these figures were higher than actual Luftwaffe losses. The RAF complained than on some occasions that British aircraft flew over the evacuation areas they were fired at by friendly anti-aircraft batteries, particularly from the ships. Misidentification was however not confined to the surface, as during the operations to protect the evacuation Spitfires on a number of occasions attacked Hurricanes.

20-22 May 1940: Following its stand-down following the losses of the 13th, No.264 Squadron flew no operational sorties until the 20th, when S/Ldr. Hunter, F/Lt. Cooke, F/Lt. Whitehouse and P/O Barwell flew a night "sector Recco". Night flying sector Recco's were conducted by P/O Whitehouse, P/O Stokes and Sgt. Thorn on the 21st as the squadron prepared for operational flying proper. On the 22nd the squadron was issued orders to commence operations from RAF Manston from the following day.

23 May 1940: In the morning 264 Squadron flew its Defiants from Duxford to Manston from where it was to fly patrols. Two patrols were flown; one in the afternoon and one in the evening. At 13.30 hours 12 Defiants took off from Manston with orders to patrol Dunkirk – Calais – Boulogne. The aircraft and crews were: L6973 (S/Ldr. Hunter/LAC King), L6959 (P/O Stokes/LAC Fairbrother), L7003 (P/O Young/LAC Johnson), L6964 (P/O Barwell/P/O Williams), L6975 (F/Lt. Cooke/Cpl. Lippett), L6961 (P/O Whitley/LAC Turner), L6972 (F/Lt. Whitehouse/P/O Scott), L6963 (P/O Kay/LAC Jones), L7007 (P/O McLeod/LAC Cox), L6967 (P/O Welsh/LAC Hayden), L6986, (P/O Hickman/LAC Fidler) and L6960 (Sgt. Lauder/P/O Hatfield). The squadron landed back at 17.30 after encountering enemy Me.110's.

The second patrol of the day was similar to the first, but was conducted in company with two Squadrons of Hurricanes. The Defiants took off from Manston at 18.40: The aircraft and crews were: L6973 (S/Ldr. Hunter/LAC King), L6975 (F/Lt. Cooke/Cpl. Lippett), L7003 (P/O Young/LAC Johnson), L6959 (P/O Stokes/LAC Fairbrother), L6964 (P/O Barwell/P/O Williams), L6961 (P/O Whitley/LAC Turner), L6972 (F/Lt. Whitehouse/P/O Scott), L6963 (P/O Kay/LAC Jones), L6967 (P/O Welsh/LAC Hayden), L6956 (P/O Hackwood/LAC Lille), L7007 (P/O McLeod/LAC Cox) and L6968 (Sgt. Lauder/P/O Hatfield). The squadron landed back at 20.40 hours.

The details and narrative of the patrol report are laid out in the Squadron Combat Report to Fighter Command for 23 May 1940 reproduced below verbatim:

F.C.C.R/75/40.   **FORM "F"**   SECRET.

FIGHTER COMMAND COMBAT REPORT.

To: **FIGHTER COMMAND.**

From No. 12 Group

THE FOLLOWING REPORT HAS BEEN RECEIVED FROM OFFICER COMMANDING R.A.F. STATION DUXFORD:

Account of patrols carried out by O.C. 264 Squadron on 23rd May 1940.
The Squadron took off from Duxford for Manston, 14 A/C including 2 reserves, at 0915 hours on 23.5.40 arriving Manston approximately 0945 hours. On landing it was seen that aircraft were bunched together along the road throughout the camp. I taxied to various points where aircraft were, and as nobody seemed to know where I should go to position my aircraft I decided to disperse my aircraft on the only clear side I could find. Petrol bowsers arrived about 20 minutes later and refueling was commenced. I went to the operations room and we were placed at 14 minutes availability. The following order "Patrol Abbeville, Doullens, Arras" no height given. These orders were cancelled almost immediately. About 20 minutes later I was ordered to stand by for escorting civil aircraft to Merville, where it was presumed these aircraft were to land and return. I was informed that I must expect very accurate anti-aircraft fire on line immediately Armentières Bethume, and between Frages and Auchel. These orders were cancelled shortly afterwards. I was ordered to remain at a state of availability.
There was no telephone communication nearer than the other end of the aerodrome almost a mile away, and so I stationed a reserve pilot at this

telephone to pass any messages. At about 1440 I received the following message: - "264 patrol Dunkirk, Calais, Boulogne, relieving 54 Squadron from Hornchurch, who are at present patrolling that area" Landfall was made at Calais at about 5,000 feet. Patrol carried out to Cape Griz Nez, Boulogne and back to Calais, to Gravelines where we turned owing to bad weather. At Calais message was received from Foster. That enemy fighters were over Dunkirk (no height given). We flew towards Dunkirk and when over Gravelines we saw seven Me.110's in search formation (changing position the whole). On sighting the enemy I gave orders to engage and turned towards them.

The enemy had a height advantage of at least 1,000 feet. We manoeuvred for position for at least 10 minutes but at 10,000 feet enemy disappeared into the clouds. (It should be noted here than in spite of having 12 aircraft to manoeuvre we appeared to climb as fast as the enemy). I kept my formation below the clouds and waited. Eventually one Me.110 came down, throttled right back and just out of range, obviously intending to commit me to a stern chase, treating us as Hurricanes, because obviously from the previous manoeuvres they appeared to be trying to get on our tails. I refused to be drawn, and shortly afterwards 6 Me.110 came out of the clouds and when they found us still in squadron formation they sheered off and climbed back into the clouds in the direction of Germany. We completed our patrol according to orders and landed Manston 1720 hours.

At 1730 hours I was warned to be ready to take off at 1900 hours to escort bombers who were going to bomb the forts at Boulogne which was reported to be in enemy hands. At 1825 hours I was ordered to be off the ground at 1830 and patrol Boulogne. By accident I discovered 2 Squadrons of Hurricanes were also carrying out the same patrol. We were given no orders as to the height or any other information. On arriving at Boulogne I saw 10 to 12 naval vessels, some of them apparently cruisers. As we approached these vessels were engaging 3 Ju.88's with anti-aircraft fire. One cruiser was hit amidships, was on fire, and apparently sank. The Ju.88's were 6 to 7 miles away going hard back towards Germany, so I considered it my job to remain on patrol. Two cruisers then made a dart for the harbor and appeared to tie up alongside.

At 2000 hours we left our patrol line as we had exceeded our time on patrol, and the Hurricanes had already left.

I brought the Squadron back to Duxford but was unable to detail an aircraft to land at Biggen Hill as ordered (illegible word) Manston just before taking off, owing to bad R/T communication, largely due to atmospherics and what appeared to be extensive jamming.

FC/S. 17570.   T.O.R. 0158.   24.5.40.

24 May 1940: The Squadron was ordered to conduct patrols of Dunkirk-Calais-Boulogne during the morning and afternoon. At 11.25 am 12 Defiants took off from Manston. Aircraft and crews were: L6973 (S/Ldr. Hunter/LAC King), L6975 (F/Lt. Cooke/Cpl. Lippett), L7003 (P/O Young/LAC Johnson), L6959 (P/O Stokes/LAC Fairbrother), L6964 (P/O Barwell/P/O Williams), L6961 (P/O Whitley/LAC Turner), L6972 (P/O Whitehouse/P/O Scott), L6963 (P/O Kay/LAC Jones), L6968 (P/O Welsh/LAC Hayden), L6967 (P/O Hickman/LAC Fidler), L7007 (P/O McLeod/LAC Wise) and L6986 (Sgt. Lauder/P/O Hatfield). The Squadron landed back at Manston at 13.05 pm.

Form 540 states that a second patrol was flown from Manston in the afternoon; however, Form 541 lists only the details for the morning patrol. However, there were two 11 Group Intelligence Reports, reproduced below verbatim, for 264 Squadron. The first is for the morning patrol and the second for the afternoon patrol not listed in the Squadron Form 541.

Defiants would fly composite patrols over the continent in company with either or Hawker Hurricane I and Supermarine Spitfire I fighters. This Spitfire I is seen in May 1940.

F.C.C.R/22/1940. FORM "F" SECRET.

FIGHTER COMMAND COMBAT REPORT

To: FIGHTER COMMAND

From No. 11 Group Intelligence

Composite Report.

12 Defiants 264 Squadron took off from Manston on patrol Calais-Boulogne. They report having encountered A.A. fire from 3 destroyers lying off Calais presumed British and the fire continued in spite of the 2 star cartridges being fired by the Defiants. The Defiants were flying at 6/7000 feet. Accurate intense A.A. fire was encountered over Boulogne and this is presumed to be German. The bursts were about 2000 feet above first section but quickly corrected for rear sections. Whilst just inland of Calais one Me. 110 was seen flying about 2000 feet above Defiants who were flying at 7000 feet stepped down to about 4000 feet. The leader climbed to attack and the gunner got in a burst whereupon the Me. 110 dived down the line of Defiants and let off a red parachute flare. No other Me. 110 appeared but the Me. 110 was attacked by several of the Defiants and finally the aircraft was set on fire by F/Lt. Whitehouse, pilot and P/O Scott gunner. Before reforming Sqdn formation about 8 or 9 Me. 109's were seen flying in vics of 3, one of which was attacked by a Defiant without result. Combat reports will be made out at home station Duxford. Although a certain amount of return cannon fire appeared to come from the Me. 110 the tactics of the pilot appeared to be poor. Weather fine with cloud. The oil refinery or deposit at Calais was seen to be on fire.
The Defiants landed Manston at 1315 hours, all pilots and aircraft serviceable.

R. 1608   24.5.40.

Ref: FC/S. 17570/INT.

FCCR/49/40.   FORM "F"   SECRET.

FIGHTER COMMAND COMBAT REPORT

To: FIGHTER COMMAND

From No. 11 Group

Composite report received from Manston.

11 Defiants of 264 Squadron took off on Patrol Boulogne, Dunkirk, and patrolled at 7/12000 feet. Weather and visibility good with thin cloud at 8000 feet. E. of Calais about 12 Me.109's were seen with one Me.110 which went in and out of the thin cloud obviously acting as decoy. The Defiants dept formation and E/A then went into cloud and were lost. Whilst in sight of Me.109's German speech was heard on same frequency on the Defiants. 1 Ju.88 was seen W. of Dunkirk flying at about 9000 feet, but on sighting the Defiants dived to about 6000 feet and flew S.E. Red Section gave chase and appeared to be slowly overhauling the E/A, but when over Roulers area and the E/A not within range the Defiants decided to return. No other E/A seen. Oil refinery at Calais seen on fire.
Defiants landed 1730 hours. No enemy casualties. All aircraft serviceable.

FC/S. 17570   T.O.R. 2131, 24.5.40.

25 May 1940: The Squadron conducted two patrols of Dunkirk-Calais-Boulogne. The first patrol led by S/Ldr. Hunter and consisting of 11 Defiants, L6973, L6956, L7003, L6959, L6967, L6961, L6963, L6968, L7007 and L6986, took off from Manston at 13.05 hours, landing at 15.05. The second patrol, again led by S/Ldr. Hunter and also consisting of 11 Defiants, L6973, L6975, L7003, L6959, L6967, L6986, L6972, L6963, L6961, L6957 and L7007, took off from Manston at 17.10 hours, landing at 19.10. No enemy aircraft were engaged in either patrol.

F.C.C.R/73/40.   FORM "F"   SECRET.

FIGHTER COMMAND COMBAT REPORT

To: FIGHTER COMMAND

From No. 11 Group

Composite report: 12 Defiants 264 Squadron took off from Manston at 1725 hrs. to patrol Dunkirk – Calais. All a/c landed 1925 and are serviceable. One a/c presumed to be a Me. 110 was seen off Dunkirk but this went into cloud and was lost. Intense A.A. fire was seen near Cassel and Hazebruck. Floods were observed at Yeurne and in area S.E. Dunkirk and Ostend. A pall of smoke appeared to come from Roubaix and Villette. About 6 transport ships and 2 destroyers were observed off Dunkirk. Patrol carried out at 10,000 ft. and no troop movements were observed.

R. 2159 25.5.40

FC/S. 17570/INT.

Note: The above Fighter Command Composite Report does not tie up with Squadron records, particularly in regards to timings.

26 May 1940: Twelve Defiants (From 541 lists only 11 and Defiant L6968 is listed twice, leaving only ten serial numbers), L6973, L6975, L6959, L7003, L6964, L7004, L6972, L6963, L7007 and L6968, led by S/Ldr. Hunter, took off from Manston at 12.20 hours with orders to patrol Dunkirk-Calais as part of the protection of an ammunition convoy proceeding from Dover to Dunkirk. When over the French coast S/Ldr. Hunter took Red Section down to investigate "a concentration of enemy tanks and transports near CALAIS". The Defiants were subjected to heavy anti-aircraft fire, although no aircraft were hit. The Squadron returned to Manston and landed at 14.05.

At 17.00 11 Defiants, L6973, L6975, L6959, L7003, L6964, L7004, L6972, L6963, L6968, L6967 and L6971, led by S/Ldr. Hunter, took off from Manston to patrol Dunkirk which was cloud covered, landing at 18.50; no enemy aircraft being encountered.

27 May 1940: Two patrols were flown over the Dunkirk-Calais area. In the first patrol 12 Defiants (Form 541 lists only 11), L6973 (S/Ldr. Hunter/LAC King), L7005 (F/Lt. Cooke/Cpl. Lippett), L6959 (P/O Stokes/LAC Fairbrother), L7003 (P/O Young/LAC Johnson), L6964 (P/O Welsh)/LAC Hayden), L7004 (P/O Whitley/LAC Turner), L6972 (F/Lt. Whitehouse/P/O Scott), L7007 (P/O McLeod/P/O Hatfield), L6957 (P/O Barwell/P/O Williams), L6986 (Sgt. Thorn/LAC Barker) and L6953 (Sgt. Lauder/LAC Revill), took off from Manston at 08.30 hours. Early in the patrol the squadron encountered Me.109's, two of which were claimed shot down. Form 540 states that later a formation of 12 He.111's was attacked, the He.111's breaking formation. Three were claimed as shot down and a further two claimed as probably shot down or at least badly damaged. However, the 11 Group Combat Intelligence Report for the Squadron states that the He.111's were attacked in the second patrol listed below. The patrol landed back at Manston at 10.20.

The second patrol took off from Manston at 11.20 hours, consisted of 12 Defiants; L6973 (S/Ldr. Hunter/LAC King), L7005 (F/Lt. Cooke/Cpl. Lippett), L6959 (P/O Stokes/LAC Fairbrother), L7003 (P/O Young/LAC Johnson), L6964 (P/O Welsh)/LAC Hayden), L7004 (P/O Whitley/LAC Turner), L6972 (F/Lt. Whitehouse/P/O Scott), L7007 (P/O McLeod/P/O Hatfield), L6957 (P/O Barwell/P/O Williams), L6967 (P/O Hickman/LAC Fidler), L6953 (Sgt. Lauder/LAC Revill) and L6986 (Sgt. Thorn/LAC Barker). A Ju.88 was attacked, but escaped and the He.111's mentioned above were engaged.

The 264 Squadron 'Fighter Command Combat Reports for the day are reproduced below verbatim:

F.C.C.R/75/40.　　　　　　　**FORM "F"**　　　　　　　**SECRET.**

FIGHTER COMMAND COMBAT REPORT

To: FIGHTER COMMAND

From No. 12 Group

(A) Sector Serial No.　　　　**G.1.**
(B) Serial No. of Order detailing Flight or Squadron to patrol NOT
　　　　　　　　　　　　　　　　　　　　　　　　KNOWN
(C) Date　　　　　　　　**27.5.40.**
(D) Flight　Squadron　　**264**
(E) Number of Enemy Aircraft　　　　**8 plus 3 unknown**

(F) Type of Enemy Aircraft   Me.109.   HE. 112

(G) Time attack was delivered   0915 hours

(H) Place attack was delivered   Between Dunkirk and Calais,

(J) Height of enemy   9,000 feet.

(K) Enemy Casualties   Conclusive... 2   Inconclusive... 1

(L) Our Casualties – Aircraft   NIL

                    Personnel   NIL

(N) (i) Searchlights (Did they illuminate enemy   N/A

     If not were they in front or behind target)

     (ii) Anti-aircraft guns (Did shell bursts assist   N/A

     pilot in intercepting the enemy).

(P) Range at which fire was opened in each attack on the enemy together with estimated length of burst.

     Red 1 -- 2 burst at 300 yards -- 50 rounds.

     Red 2 -- 1 burst 150 – 200 yards 40 rounds.

     Red 3 – 1 burst 150 – 200 yards 20 rounds.

     Blue 3 – 1 burst 300 yards, 20 rounds.

(R)	PILOTS.	GUNNERS.
	Red 1 -- S/Ldr. Hunter.	L.A.C. King.
	Red 2 – P/O Stokes	L.A.C. Fairbrother.
	Red 3 – P/O Young	L.A.C. Thompson.
	Blue 3 – P/O Welsh.	L.A.C. Hayden.

Squadron was ordered to patrol Dunkirk-Calais. At approximately 0915 hours a formation of 8 Me.109's was sighted at 9,000 feet south of Dunkirk. The Squadron was at once ordered to engage in line astern. Enemy aircraft used evading tactics by using cloud formations as cover and 2 enemy aircraft made beam attacks from cover with shell guns.

A general engagement ensued. One enemy aircraft went down in flames after two burst of 50 rounds at 300 yards by Red 1

A second went down out of control with smoke pouring from it after one burst of 40 rounds from 150 yards to 200 yards from Red 3. This aircraft had attempted a beam attack on Red 2. Three other aircraft were seen close to the formation of M.E.'s and appeared to be He. 112's but were camouflaged to look like Spitfires. No Spitfires were known to be operating in this area at the time. Just before engaging the enemy, S/Ldr. Hunter heard German on his R/T.

R.   1808   28.5.40.

Ref: FC/S.   17570/INT.

F.C.C.R/75/40. FORM "F" SECRET.

FIGHTER COMMAND COMBAT REPORT

To: FIGHTER COMMAND

From No. 12 Group, Intelligence.

(A) Sector Serial No. G.1.
(B) Serial No. of Order detailing Flight or Squadron to patrol ......
(C) Date 27.5.40.
(D) Flight Squadron 264
(E) Number of Enemy Aircraft 12
(F) Type of Enemy Aircraft He.111
(G) Time attack was delivered 1230 hours
(H) Place attack was delivered Dunkirk
(J) Height of enemy 7,000 feet.
(K) Enemy Casualties Conclusive... 3 Inconclusive... 2
(L) Our Casualties – Aircraft NIL
  Personnel NIL
(N) (i) Searchlights (Did they illuminate enemy N/A
  If not were they in front or behind target)
  (ii) Anti-aircraft guns (Did shell bursts assist N/A
  pilot in intercepting the enemy).
(P) Range at which fire was opened in each attack on the enemy together with estimated length of burst.
  Red 1... Point Blank.
  Red 2 ... 250 yards. 1 burst 200 rounds.
  Red 3 ... Not stated.
  Blue 1 ... Not stated.
  Blue 2 ... 100 yards 1 burst 500 rounds
  Blue 3 ... 150 yards 1 burst
  Yellow 1 . 150 – 200 yards. 60 yards 3 bursts.
  Yellow 2. 400 yards 1 burst 25 rounds.

(R) The Sqdn operating from Manston was ordered to patrol Calais-Dunkirk. At 1250 hours when over Dunkirk at 17,000 feet 12 He. 111's were sighted at approximately 7,000 feet. Squadron attack was ordered with Green Section instructed to remain above combat as protection against possible intervention by enemy fighters.

Attack was made from the sun, but when sighted E/A used evasive tactics, some diving towards sea-level, others diving for cloud cover, the formation breaking up. Individual combats resulted, and three E/A went down in flames, two others also went down out of control, but final result could not be seen. No enemy fighter action materialised. Rear gun fire from E/A was very poor and erratic, and very little fire was experienced from enemy lower rear gun position. Return fire also appeared to be incendiary. The attack made by the Defiants which proved most successful consisted of positioning a/c underneath the wings slightly forward of the E/A. In the case of Red 1 and Red 3, Red 1 was slightly under the port wing with Red 3 under the starboard. Visibility was good.

Red 1	... Pilot S/Ldr. Hunter.	Gunner LAC. King.
Red 2	... Pilot P/O Stokes.	Gunner LAC. Fairbrother.
Red 3	... Pilot P/O Young.	Gunner LAC. Thompson.
Blue 1	... Pilot F/Lt. Cooke.	Gunner Cpl. Lippett.
Blue 2	... Pilot P/O Whitley	Gunner LAC Turner
Blue 3	... Pilot P/O Webb.	Gunner LAC Hayden.
Yellow 1	... Pilot F/Lt. Whitehouse.	Gunner P/O Scott
Yellow 2	... Pilot P/O McLeod.	Gunner P/O Hatfield.

R. 1751   28.5.40.

Ref: FC/S. 17570/INT.

28 May 1940: Twelve Defiants (Form 541 lists only 10), L6973 (S/Ldr. Hunter/LAC King), L7005 (F/Lt. Cooke/Cpl. Lippett), L7003 (P/O Young/LAC Johnson), L7004 (P/O Whitley/LAC Turner), L6956 (Sgt. Thorn/LAC Barker), L6959 (F/Lt. Whitehouse/P/O Scott), L6963 (P/O Kay/LAC Jones), L6970 (P/O Hackwood/LAC Lille), L7007 (P/O McLeod/P/O Hatfield) and L6953 (Sgt. Daisley/LAC Revill), took off from Manston at 11.40 hours. The squadron was ordered to patrol Dunkirk and early on in the patrol encountered an estimated 27 Me.109's. In the Ensuing combats 6 Me.109's were claimed destroyed and three Defiants were shot down. The Squadron landed at 12.55. The Defiants that were shot down were L6959 (F/Lt. Whitehouse/P/O Scott), L7007 (P/O McLeod/P/O Hatfield) and L6953 (Sgt. Daisley/LAC Revill). Other squadron members observed three parachutes landing in the sea.

At 15.45 nine Defiants, L6973 (S/Ldr. Hunter/LAC King), L7005 (F/Lt. Cooke/Cpl. Lippett), L7003 (P/O Young/LAC Johnson), L7004 (P/O Whitley/LAC Turner), L6956 (Sgt. Thorn/LAC Barker), L6975 (P/O Barwell/P/O Williams), L6963 (P/O Kay/LAC Jones), L6967 (P/O Hickman/LAC Fidler) and L6970 (P/O Hackwood/LAC Lille), took off from Manston to patrol Dunkirk. No enemy aircraft were noted and the Defiants landed at 17.05.

This 264 Squadron Defiant suffered severe damage to the elevators after being attacked by a German fighter over Dunkirk on 29 May 1940. RAF

29 May 1940: At 14.30 twelve Defiants, L6973 (S/Ldr. Hunter/LAC King), L7005 (F/Lt. Cooke/Cpl. Lippett), L7004 (P/O Whitley/LAC Turner), L6967 (P/O Young/LAC Johnson), L6964 (P/O Welsh/LAC Hayden), L6975 (P/O Stokes/LAC Fairbrother), L7006 (P/O Barwell/P/O Williams), L6957 (P/O Kay/LAC Jones), L6968 (P/O Hickman/LAC Fidler), L6970 (P/O Hackwood/LAC Lille), L6956 (Sgt. Thorn/LAC Barker) and L6972 (Sgt. Lauder/LAC Wise), took off from Manston to patrol Dunkirk. The squadron encountered several formations of enemy aircraft and claimed to have destroyed 18 before returning to base and landing at 16.25; L6957 being badly damaged.

A second patrol of Dunkirk was ordered and twelve Defiants, L6973 (S/Ldr. Hunter/LAC King), L7005 (F/Lt. Cooke/Cpl. Lippett), L7004 (P/O Whitley/LAC Turner), L6967 (P/O Young/LAC Johnson), L6964 (P/O Welsh/LAC Hayden), L6975 (P/O Stokes/LAC Fairbrother), L7006 (P/O Barwell/P/O Williams), L6961 (P/O Kay/LAC Cox), L6968 (P/O Hickman/LAC Fidler), L6970 (P/O Hackwood/LAC Lille), L6956 (Sgt. Thorn/LAC Barker) and L6972 (Sgt. Lauder/LAC Wise), took off from Manston at 18.55. This patrol intercepted an enemy formation claimed to consist of about 40 Ju.87's and 3 Ju.88's; 18 Ju.87's and one Ju.88 being claimed as destroyed in the ensuing combats. One of the Defiants, L6956 (Sgt. Thorn/LAC Barker), suffered severe damage, but made it back to Manston; the Squadron landing at 20.40.

It should be noted that this total of 37 enemy aircraft claimed destroyed by 264 Squadron on this date is considered to be heavily inflated possibly by several pilots making claims for the same aircraft: i.e.: 4 Defiant engage a Ju.87, all claiming it destroyed, therefore 4 kills are claimed for one aircraft destroyed. German records clearly show that only 14 aircraft were lost to all causes on the front on 29 May 1940. Several other Squadrons also made claims on this date as did ground defences. It is probable that many of the Ju.87's claimed destroyed made it home with varying degrees of damage as the German Situation Reports for the 29th stated that the dive bombers had suffered heavily.

The 264 Squadron narrative for 29 May 1940 is reproduced below verbatim:

"S/Ldr. Hunter and twelve Defiants patrolled DUNKIRK – CALAIS in conjunction with three Hurricane Squadrons. We were detailed to look for enemy bombers with one of the Hurricane squadrons leaving the remainder to engage the fighters. The squadron was, however, attacked first by six Me.109's, two of which were destroyed and after the squadron had reformed it was attacked by twenty-one Me.110's. Fifteen of the enemy were shot down and also a Ju.87 which was brought down by Sgt. Thorn and L.A.C. Barker who were momentarily detached from the squadron. P.O. Kay's machine was badly damaged by an Me.109 and his gunner, L.A.C. Jones, baled out when the turret was hit. P.O. Kay successfully landed his machine at MANSTON. In the evening the squadron made a second patrol and engaged about forty Ju.87's and three Ju.88's which were bombing Dunkirk. Eighteen Ju.87's were destroyed and one Ju.88. Sgt. Thorn's machine was very badly damaged and had to land with one wheel stuck down. The Squadron remained at MANSTON for the night."

Following the days operations the Squadron received the following message from No.11 Group:

"The Air Officer Commanding sends sincere congratulations to No.264 Squadron on their magnificent performance in shooting down over thirty enemy aircraft today without losing a single pilot, one of whom brought back his aeroplane minus both elevators and one aileron."

The Ju.87 dive bombers proved to be extremely vulnerable to attack by British fighters including the Defiant I. Although the claims of 29 May are much higher than actual German losses, the German Situation Reports for the day stated that the dive bombers had suffered heavily.

A line of British soldiers wade out towards a Royal Navy Destroyer off Dunkirk at the height of Operation Dynamo.

Previous page top: A Royal Navy Destroyer arrives at Dover with troops evacuated from Dunkirk. Previous page bottom: A Paddle Steamer tows a line of small vessels during the evacuation from Dunkirk on 3 June 1940.

This page: A Lockheed Hudson from No.220 Squadron RAF Coastal Command conducts a reconnaissance along the coast at Dunkirk during the evacuation of the British Expeditionary Force.

            PERSONAL   **COMBAT REPORT**

Sector Serial No...(A)   **G 16**

Serial No. of Order detailing Flight or Squadron to
    Patrol..(B)   —

Date...(C)   **29/5/40**

Flight, Squadron..(D)   **Flight: A   Sqdn 264**
                                                                         One.

Number of Enemy Aircraft........................(E)

Type of Enemy Aircraft...........................(F)   **6 Me.109's ? Me.110's**

Time Attack was Delivered.......................(G)   **14.30**

Place Attack was Delivered.......................(H)   **.... Dunkirk**

Height of Enemy....................................(J)   **12,000 ft.**

Enemy Casualties...................................(K)   **1 Me.109 & 1 Me.110**

Our Casualties.............Aircraft...............(L)   **Nil**

                Personnel.............(M)   **Nil**

GENERAL REPORT...........................(R)

Searchlights. Did they illuminate target. If not   **N/A**
were they in front or behind target.

A.A GUNS. Did shell bursts assist pilot in   **No**
Identifying enemy

Range at which fire was opened in each   **150 yds 4 sec**
attack. Estimated length of bursts.   **250 yds 20 sec**

GENERAL REPORT.

We were patrolling Dunkirk... Yellow Section. At app 14.30 we were attacked by 6 Me.109's. One Me.109 flew overhead and was shot down by my Gunner LAC Hayden With a very short burst at... 150 yds...

Note: There is more to this combat report. However, it is hand written and its condition very poor and faint with much of the text illegible.

                      Signature..................

                      Section

        OC   Flight

                      Squadron   Squadron No.

The above Combat Report was submitted by P/O Welsh/LAC Hayden in Defiant I L6964

No. 264 Squadron Commanding Officer, Squadron Leader Hunter (at left of photograph) briefs 264 Squadron crews at RAF Duxford on 31 May 1940; the last day the Squadron flew Defiants over France in the day fighter role. RAF

30 May 1940: The Squadron returned to RAF Duxford; no operational sorties were flown.

31 May 1940: Two patrols were flown. The first patrol consisting of 12 Defiants, L6973 (S/Ldr. Hunter/LAC King), L6975 (F/Lt. Cooke/Cpl. Lippett), L7019 (P/O Stokes/LAC Fairbrother), L6961 (P/O Whitley/LAC Tuner), L6980 (P/O Young/LAC Johnson), L6968 (P/O Hickman/LAC Fidler), L6972 (P/O Barwell/P/O Williams), L6970 (P/O Hackwood/LAC Lille), L6963 (P/O Kay/LAC Hayden), L6953 (Sgt. Lauder/LAC Wise), L6966 (Sgt. Thorn/LAC Barker) and L6964 (P/O Thomas/LAC Cox), took off from Manston at 13.45 to patrol Dunkirk along with two other squadrons, 1 Hurricane (111Squadron) and 1 Spitfire (609 Squadron).

The patrol encountered a large formation of enemy aircraft and claimed 4 Me.109's destroyed. On the debit side three Defiants were lost; L6961 (P/O Whitley/LAC Tuner) and L6980 (P/O Young/LAC Johnson) colliding in the air. L6961 force landed in the area of Dunkirk, while L6980 crashed, the pilot parachuting clear. L6968 (P/O Hickman/LAC Fidler) was shot down, both crew being reported missing. The rest of the Squadron aircraft landed at 15.05.

The second patrol of the day, like the previous one, was a composite patrol involving Hurricanes (111 Squadron), Spitfires (609 Squadron) and Defiants of 264 Squadron. Nine Defiants, L6973 (S/Ldr. Hunter/LAC King), L6975 (F/Lt. Cooke/Cpl. Lippett), L7019 (P/O Stokes/LAC Fairbrother), L6970 (P/O Hackwood/LAC Lille), L6963 (P/O Kay/LAC Hayden), L6972 (P/O Barwell/P/O Williams), L6964 (P/O Thomas/LAC Cox), L6953 (Sgt. Lauder/LAC Wise) and L6966 (Sgt. Thorn/LAC Barker), took off from Manston at 18.35 to patrol Dunkirk at 10,000-11,000 ft, the Spitfires of 609 Squadron following behind at the same altitude while the Hurricanes of 111 Squadron were 3,000 ft above. As with the previous patrol, large numbers of enemy aircraft were encountered, five He.111's being claimed by 264 Squadron and two Defiants were lost; L6975 (F/Lt. Cooke/Cpl. Lippett) being shot down and L6972 (P/O Barwell/P/O Williams) being damaged, resulting in a forced landing in the English Channel, both crew being saved. Defiant L7019 was badly damaged, the air gunner, LAC Fairbrother, baling out after being wounded. The pilot returned to Manston but crashed. The remaining aircraft landed at Manston at 1945 hours. The other two squadrons, 111 and 609, also put in claims for these patrols, with 111 claiming 7 aircraft shot down and a further five possible during one patrol. During the first patrol 609 claimed only a single He.111 damaged, but put in several claims for enemy aircraft destroyed and damaged in the second patrol.

The 264 Squadron narrative of operations on 31 May 1940 is reproduced below verbatim:

"Squadron Leader Hunter and 11 Defiants accompanied by ten Hurricanes joined up with a squadron of Hurricanes and a squadron of Spitfires and carried out a patrol of DUNKIRK – CALAIS. The squadrons encountered about seventy Me.109's and He.111's. The enemy attacked, P.O Hickman and L.A.C. Fidler were shot down and P.O. Whitley and L.A.C. Turner and P.O. Young and L.A.C. Johnson collided in the air.
P.O's Whitley and Young and L.A.C. Turner are known to be safe in allied territory.
Four Me.109's were brought down. In the afternoon S/Ldr. Hunter and nine machines made a patrol of Dunkirk–FENNES at 18,000 feet. A squadron of Hurricanes followed behind and a squadron of Spitfires were to fly about 3,000 feet above the Defiants. A large formation of enemy fighters and bombers were met. The Hurricanes and Spitfires attacked the enemy fighters and the Defiants attacked the Heinkel 111's. Five of those machines were brought down. F/Lt. Cooke and Cpl. Lippett and P.O. Barwell and P.O. Williams were brought down. The latter two are known to be safe as they landed in an area near a British Destroyer."

The guns from L6961, which had crash landed at Dunkirk, were recovered and the wreck of the aircraft was then destroyed. The crew, P/O Whitley and LAC Tuner, arrived at RAF Manston on 1 June. P/O Young, who had jumped clear of the stricken L6980 after its collision with L6961, ended up on the ground at Dunkirk, being evacuated and disembarked at Dover on 1 June, as was P/O's Barwell and 'Williams, who had force landed L6972 in the English Channel at the end of the 2nd patrol the previous day when some five miles or so from the English Coast. The cause of the forced landing was determined to be a glycol leak and the motor seizing; the crew opting to remain with the aircraft, ditching between to Destroyers that were in the area. The Defiant apparently sank very quickly after the crew got out, P/O Barwell finding P/O Williams floating in the water knocked out. They were promptly picked up by a Destroyer and landed at Dover.

Between 12 and 31 May No.264 Squadron flew 179 sorties. Twelve of these were a show of support, patrolling The Hague on 12 and 13 May, while the remaining 167 were flown over Dunkirk-Boulogne-Calais as part of Fighter Commands operations to protect Bridgehead and then the evacuation of the BEF.

The Squadron claimed 65 enemy aircraft destroyed for the loss of 14 Defiants during May, although it is clear that the number of actual losses by the Luftwaffe during these engagements was much lower.

4

264 SQUADRON OPERATIONS JUNE & JULY 1940

31 May was 264 Squadrons last day flying operations over the evacuation area? Following its heavy losses the Squadron was stood down from operations on 1 June until 08.00 hours on the 2nd. For the most part June and July were quite months, the Squadron absorbing new aircrews and conducting training, combined with limited operational flying.

Air to sea firing was conducted on the 2nd and the 3rd, on which latter date nine replacement air gunners, all New Zealanders, joined the squadron; another four arriving the following day.

On the 4th, F/Lt. Trumble arrived to take over command of 'B' Flight. This was the date that the Squadron Commander, S/Ldr. Hunter, received the DSO and F/Lt. Cooke received the DFC. On the 7th, P/O Kay received the DFC and Sgt. Thorn, Cpl. Lippett, LAC King and LAC Turner received the DFM.

On the 6th, training flights were conducted, including air to air firing at Sutton Bridge, by the new gunners allocated to 'A' Flight. Night flying training was conducted in five Defiant flights.

Operational flying re-commenced on the 7th with three night interception patrols being flown, no enemy aircraft being encountered, followed later by a further two patrols. Defiant L7004 was lost when the aircraft suffered an airborne engine failure. The crew baled-out and the aircraft crashed.

Two additional air gunners reported to the Squadron on the 9th and on the 10th six Defiants with new air gunners carried out air to air firing practice at Sutton Bridge. The following day three Defiants with new air gunners carried out air to air firing at Sutton Bridge. One of these Defiants crashed while the pilot, P/O Hutcheson, was attempting a forced landing at Duxford after the aircraft suffered an engine failure. The pilot was killed and the air gunner, LAC Robinson, injured.

On the 12th, six Defiants conducted air to air firing at Sutton Bridge. A lecture on Night Interception and Fighting was given by Air Commodore Sir Christopher Brand, who had visited the Squadron for that purpose. On the 13th, 4 Defiants were flown on Night Flying practices.

On the 16th, S/Ldr. Hunter and P/O Kay proceeded to Farnborough along with S/Ldr. Puckham of No.19 Squadron, Spitfires, for "exercises with a Messerschmitt 109 flown by S/Ldr. Wilson". During the exercises S/Ldr. Hunter flew a Defiant, N1355, fitted with a D/H Constant Speed Airscrew and used a gun camera during his mock attacks on the Me.109. The following day S/Ldr. Hunter returned to Farnborough to fit oxygen economizer to Defiant N1355.

On the 17th four Defiants were flown on Night Flying Practice, two were flown on air to air gunnery practice at Orfordness, and P/O Welsh flew a Night Sector Recco. On the 19th, four new aircrew arrived, all of which had flown around 12 hours on Defiants at Aston Down. 'A' Flight of 264 Squadron relieved No.19 Squadron, Spitfires, on Night Readiness; two Defiants flown by P/O Stokes and Sgt. Thorn flying night patrols, neither of which encountered any enemy aircraft. The following day four Defiants flown by S/Ldr. Hunter, P/O Young, P/O Stokes and Sgt. Thorn flew Night Interception Patrols, all without incident.

On the 22nd F/Lt. Feather, Chief Test Pilot with Boulton Paul arrived at Duxford to conduct tests with squadron Defiants that were fitted with D/H Constant Speed Airscrews. On the 25th, Defiant L6957, which had been brought back from Dunkirk to Manston for repairs, was delivered to 264 Squadron at Duxford.

On the 27th, three Defiants conducted air to air gunnery practice firing off Orfordness. On the 28th Red Section was scrambled at 13.00 hours to intercept reported enemy aircraft, but none were encountered. A practice interception had been flown by the Squadron at 04.00 hours. On the 29th, three Defiants conducted air to ground firing at Sutton Bridge and S/Ldr. Hunter flew a "Low Dive Bombing" practice attack on Duxford aerodrome, the results of which were described as "very satisfactory".

July commenced with 'A' Flight conducting practice low dive bombing on Duxford aerodrome on the 1st. There were no operational sorties until the 3rd of the month when S/Ldr. Hunter led eight Defiants of 'A' Flight on an interception from Satellite aerodrome 'G.I', where the Squadron had moved to earlier that day; no enemy aircraft were encountered. A single Defiant was flown on a Night Patrol, but encountered no enemy aircraft.

Defiant I's of 264 Squadron in July 1940. RAF

Boulton Paul Defiant MK.I's from No.264 Squadron being refueled, probably at Kirton-in-Lindsey in July 1940. Following the hectic air battles of May, June and July were relatively quiet for 264 Squadron. RAF

Top: 264 Squadron crews arrive at their aircraft dispersal for a sortie in July 1940. Above: 264 Squadron Defiant I's flying in a loose 'vic' formation while operating out of Kirton-in-Lindsey in late July or early August 1940. RAF

An air gunner climbs into the turret of a Defiant I at Kirton-in-Lindsey. RAF

The next few days were occupied with various tests and enhancements of equipment. On the 4th, S/Ldr. Hunter proceeded to Boulton Paul Ltd in regards to the fitting of new engines to the Defiant MK.1. On 5 July, one of the Squadrons Defiants, L6963, was delivered to Farnborough for aileron tests to be conducted by the RAE (Royal Aircraft Establishment), and S/Ldr. Hunter and P/O Young flew night test flights in order to determine if visibility through a new type of cockpit hood was satisfactory. On the 7th and 8th air gunnery practice was conducted off Orfordness and Sutton Bridge.

Operational sorties were flown on 10 July when Red Section took off on an 'interception Patrol', but failed to locate any enemy aircraft. At 20.00 hours on the 12th 'A' Flight moved to Martlesham Heath. The following day 'A' Flight flew an interception patrol and a convoy protection patrol, being relieved at Martlesham Heath by 'B' Flight at 13.00 hours. 'B' Flight returned to Duxford at 21.00 hours.

At dawn on the 14th, 'A' Flight moved to Martlesham Heath, again being relieved by 'B' Flight at 13.00; 'B' Flight returning to Duxford at 21.00, neither Flight having conducted any operational patrols. During the early morning of the 15th, 'B' Flight moved to Martlesham Heath, both sections carrying out patrols without engaging any enemy aircraft. 'B' Flight returned to Duxford at 21.00 hours. Three Defiants flying from Duxford conducted air to sea firing practice off Orfordness as the training of new air gunners continued.

Two Night Interception Patrols were flown by P/O Barwell on the 17th; no enemy aircraft being encountered during either patrol. On the 19th Convoy Protection Patrols were flown by Red and Yellow Sections. The Squadron was scheduled to move to RAF Turnhouse, Edinburgh, Scotland, but this was cancelled at 20.15 hours on the 19th as No.141 Squadron, which had moved south from Scotland with its Defiant I's, was badly mauled by German fighters earlier in the day and the decision had been taken to send 141 Squadron to Turnhouse.

On the 20th, 264 squadron flew Convoy Protection Patrols; all Sections flying patrols between dawn and 14.00 hours. A single Night Interception Patrol was flown without encountering enemy aircraft. The 21st followed a similar pattern to the 20th, with Convoy Patrols being flown between dawn and 15.00 hours and a single Night Interception Patrol being flown; all without incident.

On the 22nd, Defiant L7005 was flown to Boulton Paul at Wolverhampton to have its turret replaced. Only a single Night Interception Patrol was flown, no enemy aircraft being encountered.

On the 20th, the Squadron had been notified that it was to move to RAF Kirton-in-Lindsey, the move taking place on the 23rd. 'A' Flight moved to the satellite station Hatfield Woodhouse at 08.00 hours on the 25th, from where Red and Yellow Sections flew Convoy Patrols, returning to Kirton at 21.30 hours. At 06.00 hours on the 26th a Defiant carried out a patrol in adverse weather. One Defiant also flew a Naval Anti-Aircraft co-operation exercise at Immingham, North East Lincolnshire.

On the 27th a captured Me.110 twin-engine fighter was inspected at Farnborough by S/Ldr. Hunter and F/Lt. Ash.

On the 28th Convoy Protection Patrols were flown by Red and Blue Sections, and the Squadron flew an affiliation exercise with Vickers Wellington bombers from No.149 Squadron. An uneventful Convoy Patrol was flown by Blue Section on the 29th, and a similar patrol was flown by Yellow Section the following day.

5

141 SQUADRON OPERATIONS, JUNE, JULY AND AUGUST 1940

On 29 March 1940, 2 No.264 pilots, P/O Welsh and P/O Hackwood, preceded to 27 MU (Maintenance Unit) Shawbury and 24 MU Ternhill respectively to collect and ferry Defiant aircraft to Grangemouth for No.141 Squadron. However, the Defiants were incomplete and the pilots returned by rail to No.264 Squadron. On 4 April 1940 P/O Whitehouse from 264 Squadron ferried a Defiant to Grangemouth for No.141 Squadron, and two more Defiants were ferried by No.264 Squadron pilots from Ternhill to Grangemouth for No.141 Squadron on the 8th. As more aircraft arrived No.141 Squadron continued training as it worked up to become operational towards the end of June 1940 when it would be tasked with day and night patrols.

29.6.1940: The first operational sorties for No.141's Squadron Defiants were flown when 3 Defiants, L6983, L6988 and L7016, took off on patrol at 09.35 hours to "investigate raid Z30", landing at 10.06.

1.7.1940: One Defiant, L6997, took off at 00.37 hours to patrol 'Yellow Line' at an altitude of 18,000 ft. At 01.35 the aircraft was ordered to return, landing at 01.54.

3.7.1940: At 13.03 hours 1 Section of, Defiants, L6998, L6992 and L6989, took off on patrol. An enemy aircraft was sighted at 13.18 hours at an altitude of 15,000 ft some 3 miles from the Defiants. The enemy aircraft, the speed of which was estimated to be in excess of 300 mph, escaped after a 10 minute chase as the Defiants were unable to overhaul. The patrol landed at 15.05 hours.

Another patrol was flown at 16.25 hours; 3 Defiants, L6959, L6983 and L6992, being tasked to patrol May Island (The Isle of May) off the Forth Estuary and "investigate R.Q. and at 16.42 hours to investigate with caution X.46". No enemy aircraft were encountered and the patrol landed at 17.23

6.7.1940: At 01.10 hours a single Defiant, L6976, took off to patrol 'White Line' at an altitude of 2,000 ft, landing at 02.10.

Two Defiants, L6997 and L7014, took off at 18.37 hours with instructions to "Investigate W.4", landing back at 18.48.

8-9.7.1940: Two Defiants were involved in an accident at 15.25 hours on the 8th when P/O Orchard collided with P/O Constantine on the ground.

A single night patrol was flown over 'White Line' by Defiant L6994 from 23.58 on the 8th until 01.25 on the 9th. Another Defiant, L6887, took off at 00.15 on the 9th; patrolling 'Yellow Line', landing at 01.40. Another Defiant, L7001, took off at 02.00 to patrol 'Yellow' and 'White Line', landing at 02.45.

On the 9th the Squadron received orders for a move to the South of England, the Headquarters going to Biggin Hill and the Squadron aircraft going to West Malling where the Squadron was to fly operations from. The move commenced on the 10th, a Hannibal and a Bombay aircraft being used to ferry operational aircrews from Turnhouse to West Malling, while the bulk of the Squadron moved by train and S/Ldr. Richardson arrived at Biggin Hill. Sixteen Defiants departed Turnhouse at 2.45 on the 12th to fly to West Malling, eventually arriving at 18.59 hour in company with transport aircraft. The following day the Defiants conducted firing practice out of West Malling as the Squadron aircraft and equipment was checked prior to operations being flown. On the 13th, 2 Defiants were collected from Duxford and flown to West Malling; the crews being flown to Duxford in a Blenheim. The Squadron moved three Defiants from West Malling to Biggin Hill on the 14th to undergo "inspection and repairs".

Operational sorties from West Malling commenced on the 14th, one Section flying a sector Recce at 10.30, landing at 11.00. A Flight of Defiants took off at 18.00 to patrol West Malling, landing at 18.45 hours. On the 15th 'A' Flight conducted a patrol of West Malling and 'B' Flight conducted a Sector Recco. Bad weather on the 16th led to no operational or non-operational flying being conducted by the squadron. The squadron now had three aircraft equipped with the Constant Speed airscrew, awaiting collection from Biggin Hill – presumably these were the three aircraft moved to Biggin Hill on the 14th.

On the 17th, 3 Defiants patrolled Gravesend. The following day the Squadron aircraft moved from West Malling to Hawkinge, a time of 17.20 hours being given, but unclear if this was the departure or arrival time. 'A' Flight conducted a patrol from Hawkinge at 20.45 hours, the Defiants then returning to West Malling where they landed at 21.45 hours.

The period known as the preliminary phase of the Battle of Britain – 10 July – 12 August saw German attacks directed mainly at shipping, although some attacks were conducted against other targets including ports, notably the attack on Dover on 19 July in which No.141 Squadrons Defiants were embroiled in the defence. Aerodromes and radar stations were among the targets on 12 August; the last day of the Preliminary Phase. During the period of the Preliminary phase Fighter Command flew 18,016 day sorties during which it lost around 150 fighters, but claiming 286 German aircraft destroyed.

10-18.7.1940: During this period 141 Squadron flew 55 operational sorties on patrols, indentifying plots, convoy escort and sector recce's.

19.7.1940: The Squadron aircraft departed West Malling for Hawkinge at 08.45 hours. 'A' Flight conducted a base patrol at 10.38 hours (this patrol is not recorded in Form 541, but is detailed in Form 540).

Twelve Defiants were ordered to patrol 20 miles south of Folkestone, but only 9, L6999, L7001, L7009, L6974, L6995, L7015, L7016, L7014 and L6983, took off at 12.33. The Squadron was ordered to intercept Ju.87's bombing shipping in Dover Harbour, but the British defences had been caught on the hop and the Defiants reached the area some 15 minutes after the first reports of bombing, by which time the enemy aircraft were on their way home. While flying in the direction of Cape Griz Nez at 5,000 ft, the Defiants were 'jumped' by Me.109E's estimated at around 20 in number. Two Defiants were shot down as the German fighters attacked out of the sun, before the fight swung northwards, the Me.109's finding the Defiants to be easy targets, particularly when attacked from astern and below where the Defiants guns could not be brought to bear. The Germans had learned the Defiants strengths and weaknesses with a total of six Defiants being shot down for the loss of one Me.109 conformed shot down. Only 2 Defiants, L6999 and L7014, returned to base safely; a third, L6983, landing severely damaged. It should be noted that pilots of No.111 Hurricane Squadron reported that the Defiants shot down 4 Me.109's. 111 Squadron had been vectored to the area to support the Defiants, but were unable to assist as they were themselves embroiled in a fight with German fighters.

Aircraft lost were:

L7001   F/Lt. Louden (pilot) injured, P/O Farus (AG) uninjured
L7009   F/Lt. Donald (pilot) killed, P/O Hamilton (AG) killed
L6974   P/O Kemp (pilot) missing, Sgt. Cromree (AG) missing
L6995   P/O Howley (pilot) missing, Sgt. Currley (AG) missing
L7015   P/O Kidson (pilot) missing, Sgt. Atkins 9AG) missing
L7016   P/O Gardner (pilot) injured, Sgt. Slater 9AG) missing

The No.141 Squadron narrative for 19 July is reproduced below verbatim:

"Squadron leaves WEST MALLING for Hawkinge at 08.45 hrs 'A' Flt patrol base at 10.38 hrs. Squadron is ordered to patrol 20 miles south of FOLKESTONE at 12.30 hrs at height of 5,000 ft. 3 Aircraft fail to leave ground in time, nine only carry out patrol. They are attacked by a superior number of M.E. 109's over the English Channel. Six of our aircraft are shot down or disabled, 4 dive into the sea. P.O GRADNER, Pilot and P/O FARNES A/Gunner are picked up by aircraft. P.O. GARDNER is taken to hospital at CANTERBURY. P.O. FARNES is uninjured.

P.O.s KEMP, KIDSON, HOWLEY are presumed lost. 5 Air Gunners are also presumed lost. F/Lt. LOUDEN crashes owing to engine cut out, 200 yds from aerodrome at HAWKINGE and is injured. He is taken to CANTERBURY hospital. His Air Gunner had baled out and is safe. F/Lt DONALD crashed at DOVER and was killed, his Air Gunner P.O HAMILTON who had baled out is missing.

3 Aircraft land at HAWKINGE at 13.00 hrs. P.O MACDOUGAL is 'shot up' but returns to base. His Air Gunner, however, baled out and is now missing. Total losses are 4 pilots killed or missing Six Air Gunners missing. Squadron is now released from operations for a short period."

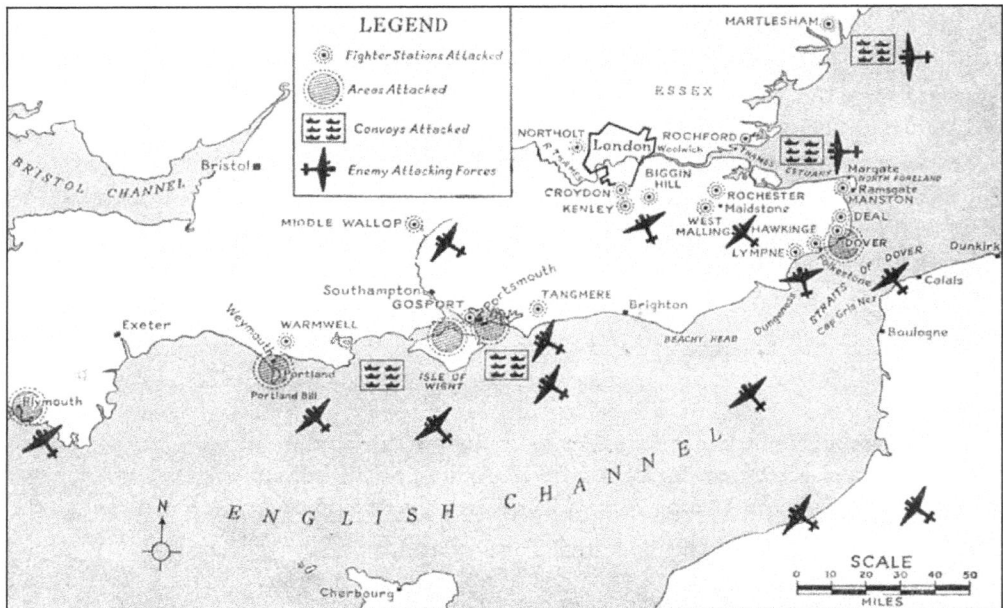

The Battle of Britain Phase I: 10 July – 18 August 1940. Attacks on South coast shipping, ports and airfields. NZTEC41

SECRET   Form "F"

PERSONAL   COMBAT REPORT

Sector Serial No...(A)   **Not given.**
Serial No. of Order detailing Flight or Squadron to
   Patrol.......................................(B)   **"   "**
Date..(C)   **19ᵗʰ July 1940.**
Flight, Squadron.....................................(D)   **Flight A&B Sqdn 141.**
Number of Enemy Aircraft........................(E)   **12**
Type of Enemy Aircraft...........................(F)   **Me.109's.**
Time Attack was Delivered......................(G)   **12.45.**
Place Attack was Delivered.....................(H)   **25 Miles south of**
                                                               Folkestone
Height of Enemy...................................(J)   **20,000 ft.**
Enemy Casualties.................................(K)   **4**
Our Casualties............Aircraft...............(L)   **6**
                      Personnel............(M)   **10**
GENERAL REPORT...........................(R)

At approximately 12.35 hours the Squadron was ordered to patrol 20 miles
South of Folkestone 5,000 feet. At 12.35 the order was received to sweep Cape
Gris Nez at 5,000 feet. The Squadron was attacked out of the sun by about 20 –
25 M.E. 109's. I immediately turned to post, (should read PORT: Author),
completing a steep turn of 360°. This proved in-effective, as A/C attacked from
below on the outside. I then carried out S turns, turning away towards the
attack, this proved effective. After 5 mins. Red 2 and myself Red 1 were the
only two Defiants left, so decided to break off the combat and returned to base.

Signature(Sgd)S/Ldr. W.A. RICHARDSON
Section
OC   Flight
Squadron   Squadron No.

Form "F"

PERSONAL   COMBAT REPORT

Sector Serial No...(A)   **Not given.**
Serial No. of Order detailing Flight or Squadron to
    Patrol.......................................(B)   "   "
Date..(C)   **19th July 1940.**
Flight, Squadron......................................(D) **Flight A and B   Sqdn 141**
Number of Enemy Aircraft........................(E)   **12**
Type of Enemy Aircraft...........................(F)   **Me.109**
Time Attack was Delivered......................(G)   **12.45**
Place Attack was Delivered......................(H)   **25 Miles south of**
    Folkestone
Height of Enemy.....................................(J)   **20,000 ft.**
Enemy Casualties....................................(K)   **4**
Our Casualties.............Aircraft................(L)   **6**
             Personnel.............(M)   **10**
GENERAL REPORT.............................(R)

Owing to the fact that Green 1 and Yellow 2 did not take off, I assumed Yellow 2's position – I followed the Squadron at 5,000 feet – I never saw any of the planes at all, during the first two attacks, but bullets were being fired at me from all angles. After the 3rd attack my engine cut and believing that I had been shot down, ordered the Air Gunner to jump, but as I got no answer assumed him killed, and decided to come down to sea level to land. On my way down my engine restarted, and I was able to precede to my base; where I found the turret empty, the Air Gunner having obviously bailed out previously.

          Signature(Sgd) I.N McDougal P/O.
          Section   'B' Flight
    OC   Flight
          Squadron   Squadron No. 141

No.141 Squadron received 7 Defiants on the 20th to replace the aircraft lost the previous day. The following day orders were issued for the Squadron to move to Prestwick, Scotland. The squadron re-commenced operational flying on the 28th when two Defiants, N1537 and N1519, took off at 14.45 and conducted a patrol of Abbotsinch at 15,000 ft, landing at 15.30. At 19.20 three Defiants, N1564, N1566 and L7011, took off to patrol Troon at 19,000 ft, landing at 20.20. On the 29th a single night patrol was conducted, Defiant L7011 taking off at 00.05 and landing at 00.25. On the 30th three Defiants, N1564, L7011 and L6994, took off at 11.55 to patrol May Island, lying in the northern outer Firth of Forth some 8 km from the mainland. The patrol was conducted at 15,000 ft with no enemy aircraft being encountered, the patrol then landing at 12.30.

During August 141 Squadron continued flying day and night patrols.

3 August 1940: 6 Day patrol sorties
6 August 1940: 3 Day patrol sorties
11 August 1940: 2 Day patrol sorties
23 August 1940: 17 Day patrol sorties
24 August 1940: 3 Day patrol sorties
25 August 1940: 6 Day patrol sorties
26 August 1940: 13 Day patrol sorties
27 August 1940: 9 Day patrol sorties
28 August 1940: 7 Day patrol sorties
29 August 1940: 3 Day interception sorties

August 66 Day sorties and 22 Night sorties

264 SQUADRON OPERATIONS 1 AUGUST - 3 SEPTEMBER 1940

1 August 1940: Eleven sorties were flown on four Convoy Patrols, L7003, L7021 and L7028 taking off at 12.00 hours and landing at 14.00 hours. L7013, N1536 and L6967 took off at 13.55 hours and landed at 15.00 hours; L6957, L7006 and L7018 took off at 16.30 and landed at 17.00; L6996 and another Defiant (the Form 541 states L6996, the same serial as the other aircraft in the section) took off at 17.05 and landed at 18.30. No enemy aircraft were encountered on these patrols.

2 August 1940: Nine sorties were flown on three Convoy Patrols. L7021, L7028 and L6973 took off at 07.30 hours and landed at 08.40; L7024 and N1536 took off at 13.05 hours and landed at 14.45; L7028, L7021 and L6996 took off at 15.00 and landed at 16.05. No enemy aircraft were encountered on these patrols.

6 August 1940: There were no operational patrols between 3 and 5 August; patrols commencing again on the 6th. Three operational sorties were flown on Convoy Patrol, N1535, L7026 and L7013 taking off at 11.40 and landing between 12.50 and 12.55. No enemy aircraft were encountered.

7 August 1940: Two convoy patrols were flown with a total of six operational sorties. N1536, L7013 and L7026 took off at 14.45 and landed at 16.35; L7006, L7025 and L7024 took off at 15.50 and landed at 17.25, no enemy aircraft being encountered on either patrol.

8 August 1940: One Convoy Patrol of three aircraft was flown, L7018, L7013 and L7006 taking off at 07.00 hours. L7018 returned at 07.20 and the other two aircraft landed at 07.45.

9 August 1940: Six operational sorties were flown in two Convoy Patrols, each of three aircraft. L7013, L7018 and L7006 took off at 09.35; L7013 returning at 09.55 with an un-noted defect, while the other two aircraft landed at 10.30. N1536, L7013 and L7025 took off at 13.50 and landed at 15.05, no enemy aircraft being encountered in either patrol.

11 August 1940: Six sorties were flown. L7003, L7005 and L7024 took off on an interception from Ringway at 16.15 hours, but were recalled without engaging any enemy aircraft, landing at 16.40. L7025, L7018 and L7027 took off on an interception at 19.00, but were recalled without engaging any enemy aircraft, landing at 19.30.

The period of the Battle of Britain referred to as the First Phase lasted from 13-23 August 1940. This phase opened with the Luftwaffe flying over 1,400 sorties attacking fighter stations and other targets in southern England on the 13th, 'Eagle Day', with Fighter Command flying around 700 day sorties, losing 13 fighters and claiming 45 German aircraft shot down. The intensity of the German attacks waxed and waned throughout the period with Fighter Command flying 6,414 day fighter sorties during the period, losing 114 fighters and claiming 290 German aircraft destroyed.

15 August 1940: L7018, L7024 and L7013 took off on a Convoy Patrol at 06.40 hours, landing at 07.50, except L7013, which landed at 06.55 after returning with a defect.

Between 13.05 and 13.10 both flights, consisting of N1535, L7003, L7021, L7028, L6973, L7027, L7018, L7024, L7006, L7026 and N1536, took off on patrol to escort a Convoy out of the Humber. No enemy aircraft were engaged, but while the Squadron was engaged in the Convoy escort, Driffield was attacked by a large formation of enemy aircraft. The Squadron landed at 14.55.

L6985, crewed by P/O Whitely (pilot) and Sgt. Turner (air gunner), took off on a night patrol at 22.35 hours. A He.111 was intercepted and engaged, but was lost in cloud. This aircraft was later confirmed destroyed. L6985 landed at 00.05 hours on the 16th.

16 August 1940: L7021 took off on a night patrol at 01.55 hours, landing at 03.05 having encountered no enemy aircraft. This was the only operational sortie flown by the Squadron on this date.

17 August 1940: Five operational sorties were flown on two convoy escort patrols. L6996 and L7027 took off at 05.10 hours and landed at 06.35 hours, having encountered no enemy aircraft. L7018, L7025 and L6957 took off at

15.05 and landed at 16.10, no enemy aircraft being encountered.

18 August 1940: N1535 took off at 03.55 hours on a night patrol, landing at 04.55, No enemy aircraft encountered. This was the only operational sortie flown by the Squadron on this date.

19 August 1940: Three operational sorties were flown on a single convoy escort patrol, L7003, L6996 and L7021 taking off at 0⁵ ᵔᵔ and landing at 06.50; no enemy aircraft encountered.

20 August 1940: Two Defiants, N1535 and L7003, took off to patrol Manston at 19.25, landing at 20.40. These were the only operational sorties flown by the Squadron on this date.

22 August 1940: The Squadron was ordered to patrol Manston. Ten Defiants, L6985, L6996 (this was probably L7021 and not L6996 as listed in Form 541), L6996 (this aircraft is listed on Form 541 twice), L7028, L6963, L7018, L7024, L7025, N1536 and L7006, took off between 19.20 and 19.25 hours. L7028 and N1536 returned at 20.05 owing to defects; L7028 force landing at Eastchurch. The rest of the Squadron landed between 20.40 and 20.45, having not engaged any enemy aircraft.

23 August 1940: The Squadron was ordered to patrol the Thames Estuary, Defiants L7003, L6985 and L7005 taking off at 07.40 hours and landing at 08.30 hours having not encountered any enemy aircraft.

The second Phase of the Battle of Britain is generally considered to have commenced on 24 August 1940, lasting until 6 September. During this period Fighter Command flew some 10.673 sorties and the Luftwaffe flew around 13,724 sorties. During this period Fighter Command lost 286 fighters and claimed 380 German aircraft shot down.

On the 19th, the German Commander in Chief issued orders that Luftflotte 2 and 3 would continue attacks designed to weaken RAF Fighter Command. Luftflotte 5 would attack Glasgow by night as well as conduct some minor attacks elsewhere. Luftflotte 3 would also be tasked with launching night attacks on targets such as Liverpool. The high attrition of the previous fighting and in particular the battles of the 15th, it was hoped, would be avoided. In 11 Group Fighter Command, Park too was hoping to avoid the high losses of previous days. It was, however, at the same time accepted that everything possible should be done to try and prevent German bombers reaching their targets. To this end he ordered that a higher proportion of his fighters would attack bombers and a smaller proportion would attack the escorting fighters. His Sector Stations he contented should be protected by fighter formations patrolling below the cloud base, at least when the stations were under serious or imminent threat. For this he demanded that reinforcements should be forthcoming from 12 Group; these being used to protect stations north of the River Thames. It was rightly determined by Park that if he could keep his Sector Stations operational then he could continue to inflict losses on the enemy, which, it was assumed would ultimately lead to victory in the battle. Parks plan to send more fighters against the bombers was to a large extent thwarted by the fact that the Germans were sending smaller formations of bombers with increased fighter escort. This meant that fighter squadrons, mainly Spitfires, were sent against the Me.109 top cover, while Hurricane and some Spitfire Squadrons would be employed against the bombers and their close escorts.

When the second phase opened on 24 August the Germans adopted a tactic of patrolling the Straits of Dover in varying degrees of strength from dusk until dawn. These enemy formations were used to mask real attacks and draw British fighters against them, leaving target areas more vulnerable. The number of Me.109's available to Luftflotte 2 increased from the 27th as Luftflotte 3 switched mainly to night attacks.

It was during this phase of the battle that No.264 Squadron was caught up in some of the heaviest fighting, suffering severe losses which contributed to Dowding's decision to withdraw it from the day fighter role and transfer it to the night fighter role at the beginning of September 1940.

24 August 1940: No.264 Squadron was ordered to patrol Manston, L6969, L7013, L7018 and N1536 taking off at 05.35 hours, landing back at 07.05. N1535, L6985, L6996 and L7027 took off at 08.00 and landed at 09.45. No enemy aircraft were engaged during these patrols.

At 08.00 Defiants L7025, L7005, N1536, L7018, L6967, L7005 (Note: L7005 is listed twice on this patrol with two separate crews; therefore, it appears that another aircraft, not listed, was part of the patrol) and L7002 took off on patrol from Manston, followed by L7013, which took of five minutes later. The patrol did not engage any enemy aircraft, but L7013, crewed by F/Lt. Colquhoun (pilot) and P/O Robinson (air gunner), was attacked by fighters reported as He.113's (this type was not operational with the Luftwaffe), but were probably Me.109's or British aircraft. L7013 was damaged, but escaped and returned to Manston at 08.30. The other Defiants landed staggered between 09.45 and 09.55.

At 11.30, Defiants N1535 (S/Ldr. Hunter/P.O King), L7003 (Sgt. Thorn/Sgt. Barker), L7005 (P/O Young/Sgt. Russell), L6966 (P/O Jones/P/O Ponting), L7027 (P/O Shaw/Sgt. Berry), L6967 (F/O Stephenson/Sgt. Maxwell, L6985 (F/Lt. Banham/Sgt. Baker), L7021 (P/O Whitley/Sgt. Turner, L7025 (S/Ldr. Garvin/F/Lt. Ash, L7018 (P/O Knocker/P/O Toombs) and L7006 (P/O Barwell/Sgt. Martin), took off to patrol Manston.

The German raids of 24 August had commenced mainly with faints and minor raids, tying up the British defences, but with no major combats. However, by around 12.20 pm the Chain Home radar stations started to pick up at least five formations of aircraft spread out from Dunkirk to Boulogne. At the time Fighter Command had one squadron, No.264, up covering RAF Manston, although this was due to be relieved by a fresh squadron, with another squadron en-route to cover Hawkinge. No.11 Groups "flanking aerodromes" of Martlesham and Tangmere were being covered by elements of two other squadrons.

The German formations headed for the Dover area, and although some of these were merely feints, one penetrated close enough for the Dover anti-aircraft guns to open fire. The main German force crossed the English coast close to Deal at a most opportune time as three sections of 264 Squadron patrolling Manston had just landed to refuel, leaving only a single section to cover the station as the relieving squadron had not yet arrived. There are conflicting accounts, with 264 Squadrons operational records showing that one section with Defiants N1535, L7003 and L7005 had landed at Manston to refuel at 12.30, around which time a formation of enemy aircraft approached to attack the station. This leaves some ambiguity as to whether three sections were on the ground and one in the air or one section on the ground and three in the air as the German bombers approached.

The German formation bombed Manston causing much damage. The nine Defiants (according to the official history) that had been refueling had only just taken off as the bombs started to fall. These Defiants, along with the 3 aircraft of the section that was covering the station then engaged the German formation, being joined a short time later by a Hurricane squadron that had been heading to Hawkinge, but redirected to assist the Defiants of 264 Squadron defending Manston.

During the course of the combats that followed the Germans lost five bombers and two Me.109's, but had successfully rendered Manston unusable for a period as the damage was so severe that the resident squadron and much of the ground staff were withdrawn, and German fighter patrols over the Straits of Dover in the few hours following the attack led to the fear, not unfounded, that another major raid on the station was imminent.

264 Squadrons operational records state that the enemy aircraft attacking Manston were engaged, during which 3 Ju.88's were shot down; one each by L6985 (F/Lt. Benham/Sgt. Baker), L7021 (P/O Whitley/Sgt. Turner) and L7025 (S/Ldr. Garvin/F/Lt. Ash), along with an enemy fighter described as an He.113, but actually an Me.109, which was shot down by L7026 (P/O Barwell/Sgt. Martin). During the initial engagement with the enemy aircraft two Defiants, L6966 and L7027, were shot down.

The three Defiants that had landed at Manston took off at 12.40, after a quick refuel, with the intention of rejoining the rest of the Squadron. A Ju.88 was destroyed by L7003 (Sgt. Thorn/Sgt. Barker), but Defiant N1535 (S/Ldr.

Hunter/P/O King) was reported missing.

Although there is clear ambiguity as to whether 3 sections were refueling or 1 section was refueling, it is clear that all 12 Defiants were engaged in the ensuing combats with the German formation. 264 Squadron had lost 3 Defiants shot down, but had claimed 4 Ju.88's and a Me.109 shot down. The action over, the Squadron landed between 13.30 and 13.35.

The second large raid just after 3.00 pm, consisting of around 50 aircraft in several formations, came in as a RAF fighter squadron was returning from covering the area following the previous raid. There were four other fighter squadrons on patrol lines on the southern and eastern approaches to London. Two of these engaged a German force attacking Manston, but were unable to prevent the station being bombed again. A third squadron attacked another German force headed for RAF Hornchurch, but were outmaneuvered by the German fighter escort and the German bombers continued towards Hornchurch despite being attacked by the Thames and Meday anti-aircraft guns and a further two RAF fighter squadrons. For the crews of 264 Squadron it was beginning to look personal as they were again on the ground at Hornchurch, as they had been at Manston earlier in the day, when the German raid came in. Seven of the squadrons Defiants were preparing to take off when the first German bombs started to drop on the station. The Defiants, however, got airborne and attacked the German force as it was retiring. There wasn't much damage to Hornchurch, with only six bombs landing in the perimeter.

No.264 Squadrons records state that the seven Defiants took off from Hornchurch as it was being bombed, but state that the time was 15.40 and not just after three as the official history record of this raid reads. At 15.40 the seven Defiants, L7025 (S/Ldr. Garvin/F/Lt. Ash), L6985 (F/Lt. Banham/Sgt. Turner), L7005 (P/O Young/Sgt. Russell), L7003 (P/O Welsh/Sgt. Hayden), N1536 (P/O Barwell/Sgt. Martin), L7024 (P/O Goodall/Sgt. Young) and L6967 (P/O Gaskell/Sgt. Machin), took off to intercept the enemy aircraft as Hornchurch was being attacked and during the ensuing combats L7025 (S/Ldr. Garvin/F/Lt. Ash) claimed 2 Ju.88's destroyed; L7005 (P/O Young/Sgt. Russell) claimed a He.111 destroyed; L7003 (P/O Welsh/Sgt. Hayden) claimed a Ju,88 and an Me.109 destroyed, while L6985 (F/Lt. Banham/Sgt. Turner) and L7024 (P/O Goodall/Sgt. Young) each claimed one half of a Ju.88 as probably destroyed, but later considered damaged. One Defiant, L6967 (P/O Gaskell/Sgt. Machin), was shot down, the air gunner being killed. Two Defiants, L7005 and L7003, landed at 16.35, L6985 landed at 16.55 and the remaining three, L7025, N1536 and L7024, landed at 17.00.

There were further raids later in the day, but 264 Squadron, which had suffered severely during the day's actions, was not involved in countering these. By the end of the days combats Fighter Command had flown 936 sorties to which was added 45 night time sorties as a heavy scale of night raids followed the day attacks.

INTELLIGENCE COMBAT REPORT

264 SQUADRON 1242 – 1330 hours

24th AUGUST 1940

264 Squadron were landing at Manston to refuel after a patrol and at 1230 hours 3 sections had landed and Yellow section were patrolling the aerodrome as a guard, when the Squadron was ordered off again to patrol Manston at 15,000 feet on the approach of a hostile raid. At 1242 hours, Red, Blue and Green sections took off to join Yellow section, but before they had time to form up over the aerodrome and gain height, the aerodrome was attacked by about 20 JU 88's approaching from the South-east.

The enemy aircraft dived at about 45 degrees to release their bombs. The Defiants were not able to overtake the enemy aircraft in their dive, but picked them up when they flattened out after the attack. A formation attack by the Defiants was impossible as the Squadron had not then joined up and a series of individual combats developed, in which our fighters in the main delivered either beam attacks or attacks from below and ahead. Very little return fire from the enemy aircraft guns was noticed.

The Defiants, using maximum boost, were unable to overtake the JU 88's without much difficulty.

Our pilots claim the following enemy casualties:-

P/O Whitley	Yellow 2	1 JU 88 destroyed.
Sgt. Turner		(Starboard wing and both engines on fire)
Sgt. Thorne	Red 2	1 JU 88 destroyed (on fire and seen by Yellow 2 to crash)
P/O Knocker	Blue 3	1 JU 88 damaged (one engine disabled)
P/O Barwell	Green 1	1 HE 113 (crashed in sea)

Our casualties

3 Defiants and crews missing.
S/Ldr Hunter and P/O King.
P/O Jones and P/O Ponting
F/O Shaw and Sgt. Berry.
1 Defiant Category 2.

INTELLIGENCE COMBAT REPORT

264 SQUADRON 1540 – 1700 hours

24th AUGUST 1940

At 1540 hours, 264 Squadron was ordered off ground to orbit base, with a view to intercepting a raid approaching Hornchurch Aerodrome from the Maidstone direction.

Seven aircraft started to take off, but before two of them were airborne, bombs had dropped in the dispersal bays they had just left.

The seven aircraft, unable to get into Squadron formation, climbed up to intercept 24 JU 88's at 10,000 feet.

One pilot saw a HE 111 at 8,000 feet apparently by itself.

This he shot down using an overtaking attack.

The other members of the Squadron started individual attacks on the rear of the formation of JU 88's which had spread out. In the ensuing combats, the pilots used a cross-over or overtaking attack.

The overtaking attacks on the JU 88's were most successful, the gunner firing back into the front of the JU 88's pilot's cockpit.

Enemy Casualties

P/O Young.	1 HE 111	Destroyed
S/Ldr Garvin	2 JU 88's	Destroyed
P/O Welsh	1 JU 88	Destroyed
F/Lt Banham	½ JU 88	Probable
P/O Goodall	½ JU 88	Probable
P/O Welsh	1 ME 109	Damaged

Our Casualties

One Defiant hit by cannon fire force landed – aircraft "write-off". Pilot safe and unhurt – gunner died of wounds in the chest.

Intelligence Officer,
RAF. Station
Hornchurch.

Defiant I's from 264 Squadron are prepared for take-off at Kirton-in-Lindsey.
RAF

25 August 1940: Ten Defiants, L7025, L6985, L7005, L7003, L7028, L7024, L7026, L7018, N1536 and L6957, took off between 19.00 and 19.05 hours to patrol Dover, landing between 20.10 and 20.15; no enemy aircraft being engaged.

26 August 1940: Three Defiants, L6985 (F/Lt. Banham/Sgt. Baker), L7028 (P/O Hughes/Sgt. Gash), L7005 (Sgt. Thorn/Sgt. Barker), took off at 11.45, followed at 11.50 by L7026 (F/Lt. Colquhoun/P/O Robinson), L7024 (P/O Goodall/Sgt. Young), L7025 (F/O Stephenson/Sgt. Maxwell) and N1536 (P/O Barwell/Sgt. Martin). The squadron was ordered to intercept enemy aircraft. Off Dover the squadron intercepted a formation of 12 Do.17 bombers escorted by Me.109's (Form 541 states Me.109's and He.113's, but the latter was not in service). During the ensuing combats 2 Do.17's were claimed destroyed by L7028 (P/O Hughes/Sgt. Gash) and 2 Do.17's and a Me.109 were claimed Destroyed by L7005 (Sgt. Thorn/Sgt. Barker). L7005 was badly damaged in the combats and force landed near Herne Bay, catching fire and being destroyed. 1 Do.17 was claimed destroyed by L7024 (P/O Goodall/Sgt. Young); L7024 suffering Cat.2 damage during the combat. 1 Do.17 was claimed as damaged by L7026 (F/Lt. Colquhoun/P/O Robinson). L7025 (F/O Stephenson/Sgt. Maxwell) was shot down, crashing into the English Channel, the Air Gunner being reported missing. L6985 was also shot down bringing 264 Squadrons losses for the day to three Defiants destroyed and 1 seriously damaged. These losses following on from the heavy losses of the 24th could not be sustained, a fact, which combined with Dowding's concerns that the Defiant could not adequately compete with the Me.109E, would see the squadron removed from the day fighter role. Following the combats the staggered elements of the squadron landed between 12.35 and 13.00.

INTELLIGENCE COMBAT REPORT

264 SQUADRON – 1200 – 1305 hours

26th AUGUST 1940

At 1142 hours, 264 Squadron was ordered to take off and patrol Dover to intercept approaching enemy bombers.

At 11,000 feet the Squadron observed a formation of 12 DO 17's in Vics line astern. The Squadron climbed up and attacked in Vics line astern from below, between Herne Bay and Deal.

While delivering their attack, they were harassed by at least 50 ME 109's, which kept on diving on them and appeared to be otherwise unengaged.

The formation of DO 17's adopted no evasive tactics but brought cross fire to bear. Fire was noticed from the side panels as well as front and rear positions.

The HE 113's were also noticed with yellow wing tips.

The Squadron landed at 1300 hours.

The following enemy casualties are claimed:-

P/O Hughes)
Sgt. Gash   )   2 DO 17's destroyed – both on fire and with pieces coming off

P/O Goodall)
Sgt. Young   )   1 DO 17 destroyed – on fire – two of the crew bailed out.

F/Lt Banham)
Sgt. Baker   )   1 DO 17 destroyed – on fire – seen to go down by Sgt. Thorne

Sgt. Thorne)
Sgt. Barker)   2 DO 17's destroyed – on fire – pieces coming off – crashed in woods near Herne Bay. 1 Me 109 destroyed (illegible handwritten)

F/Lt Colqhoun)
P/O Robinson) 1 DO 17 damaged. Broke formation – smoking from both engines.

Our casualties:- 2 Air Gunners missing – Sgt. Baker
                                                Sgt. Maxwell

                3 Defiants – Category 3

                                Intelligence Officer for
                                Group Captain Commanding
                                RAF Station
                                HORNCHURCH

Top: 264 Squadron Defiant I's at Kirton-in-Lindsey in August 1940. The aircraft nearest is N1536 (PS-R). Above: A Defiant I 'vic' formation lead by Squadron Leader Phillip Hunter in August 1940. RAF

27 August 1940: The German daylight offensive was on a much reduced scale, with few raids. Three Defiants, N1574, L7028 and N1576, took off at 18.45 to patrol the Thames Estuary, landing between 19.20 and 19.25.

28 August 1940: The Luftwaffe again increased the scale of attacks, with a number of heavy raids commencing in the morning with attacks on the airfields at Eastchurch and Rochford.

Twelve Defiants, L7021 (S/Ldr. Garvin/F/Lt. Ash), L7028 (P/O Young/Sgt. Russell), N1576 (P/O Carnaby/P/O Ellery), N1574 (P/O Whitley/Sgt. Turner), N1672 (P/O Welsh/Sgt. Hayden), N1569 (P/O Bailey/Sgt. Hardy), N1673 (F/Lt. Colquhoun/P/O Robinson), N1556 (P/O Hackwood/P/O Storrie), L6957 (Sgt. Lauder/Sgt. Chapman), L7026 (P/O Kenner/P/O Johnson), L7018 (P/O Thomas/Sgt. Shepherd) and L6963 (P/O Bowen/P/O Sutton), took off from Rochford between 08.30 and 08.35 hours to patrol off Dover. An enemy formation of around 20 He.111 bombers with a strong Me.109 escort was intercepted by the Defiants of 264 Squadron in combination with three other fighter squadrons, during which one He.111 was claimed shot down by N1576 (P/O Carnaby/P/O Ellery). The Squadron paid a high price however; four Defiants being either shot down or crashing due to damage, while four other Defiants suffered various degrees of damage, but returned to base. Defiant L7021 (S/Ldr. Garvin/F/Lt. Ash) was shot down, the crew bailing out, but F/Lt. Ash being killed; N1569 (P/O Bailey/Sgt. Hardy) was shot down, but the crew got out safely; N1574 (P/O Whitley/Sgt. Turner) suffered serious damage and crashed, the crew being killed; L7026 (P/O Kenner/P/O Johnson) suffered serious damage and crashed, the crew also being killed. L7028 (P/O Young/Sgt. Russell) suffered damage to the tail unit; N1673 (F/Lt. Colquhoun/P/O Robinson) and L6957 (Sgt. Lauder/Sgt. Chapman) both had their fuel tanks holed, and L6963 (P/O Bowen/P/O Sutton) suffered Category 2 damage.

Another two RAF fighters of the other intercepting squadrons were shot down, with claims of five German aircraft shot down, including the He.111 claimed by 264 Squadron. The Germans, however, got through and inflicted much damage on their target, the precious Coastal Command aerodrome.

Not long after noon a force of 27 German bombers with a fighter escort were headed for Rochford, being intercepted by several RAF fighter squadrons en-route, despite which they continued to their target. 264 Squadron were on the ground at Rochford, but three Defiants, N1672, N1576 and N1556, took off at 12.45 just before the station was bombed. The section was too late to intercept the enemy aircraft, landing at 13.10. Although several references are made in official histories that the entire 264 Squadron took off from Rochford just before the bombs fell, 264 Squadrons operational documentation states quite clearly that only the 1 Section of three aircraft noted above took off just before the attack, the station luckily being spared heavy damage with only a few buildings destroyed or damaged. In the defence put up by Fighter Command against this particular raid it was concluded that two German fighters and 1 bomber were shot down, but at a cost of three RAF fighters.

Two Defiants, N1672 and N1576, took off to patrol Rochford at 16.05 and landed at Hornchurch at 17.30. Three Defiants, N1628, N1581 and N1630, took off to patrol Hornchurch at 16.50, landing at 17.15. Neither of these patrols encountered enemy aircraft, but further raids during the afternoon were engaged by seven British fighter squadrons, nine British aircraft being lost, with a similar number of German aircraft thought to have been destroyed.

The RAF was at this point of the battle inflicting losses not much higher than its own and in some cases lower, the declining profit margin, combined with 264 Squadrons high loss rate over the past four days contributing to the decision to move the squadron from 11 Group back to 12 Group where it would increasingly take on a night fighter role. To all intents and purposes the Defiants time as a day fighter were at an end, although it would still fly a few Convoy protection and local defence daylight patrols with both 264 and 141 Squadrons during September.

No.264 Squadron moved to RAF Kirton-in-Lindsey, but there was no operational flying during the last three days of August or the first two days of September. On the 3rd of the month 3 sorties were flown. Defiants N1672 (P/O Welsh/Sgt. Hayden), N1558 (P/O Stokes/P/O Carlin) and N1562 (Sgt. Thorn/Sgt. Barker), took off at 14.10 hours on a Convoy Protection Patrol, landing at 14.45 not having encountered any enemy aircraft. These 3 sorties were the last daytime operational fighter sorties flown by 264 Squadrons Defiants, although a few of the night patrols flown later in the month would take-off just before sunset.

The Third Phase of the Battle from 7 September until 31 October 1940 was a period in which the Luftwaffe increasingly turned to night bombing, although many daylight operations were also conducted. The Defiants of 141 and 264 Squadron operated from various bases in the Night Fighter role and would be joined towards the end of the year by No.307 (Polish) Squadron.

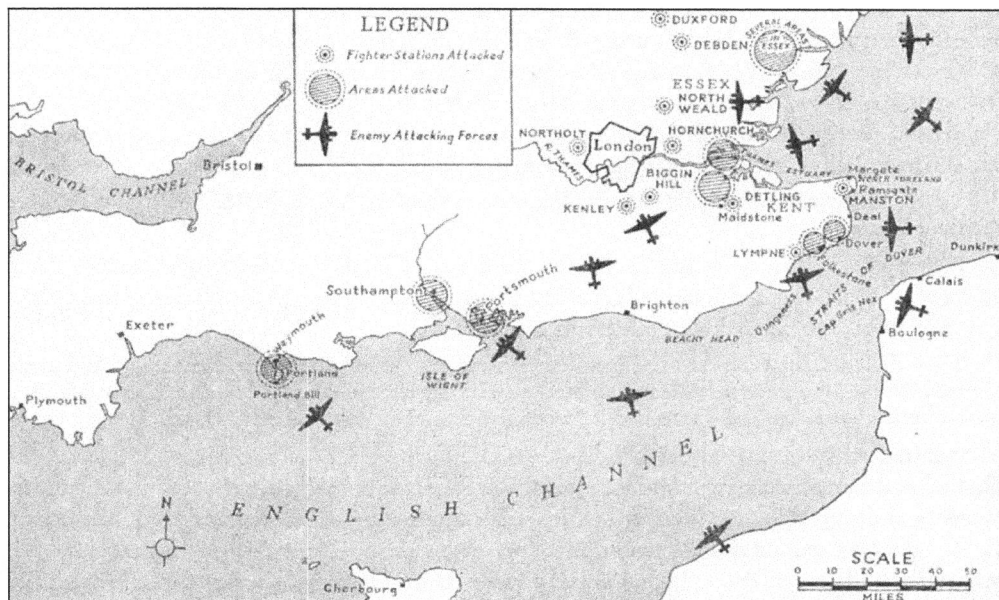

The Battle of Britain Phase II: 24 August – 6 September 1940. Luftwaffe attacks on airfields covering London. NZTEC

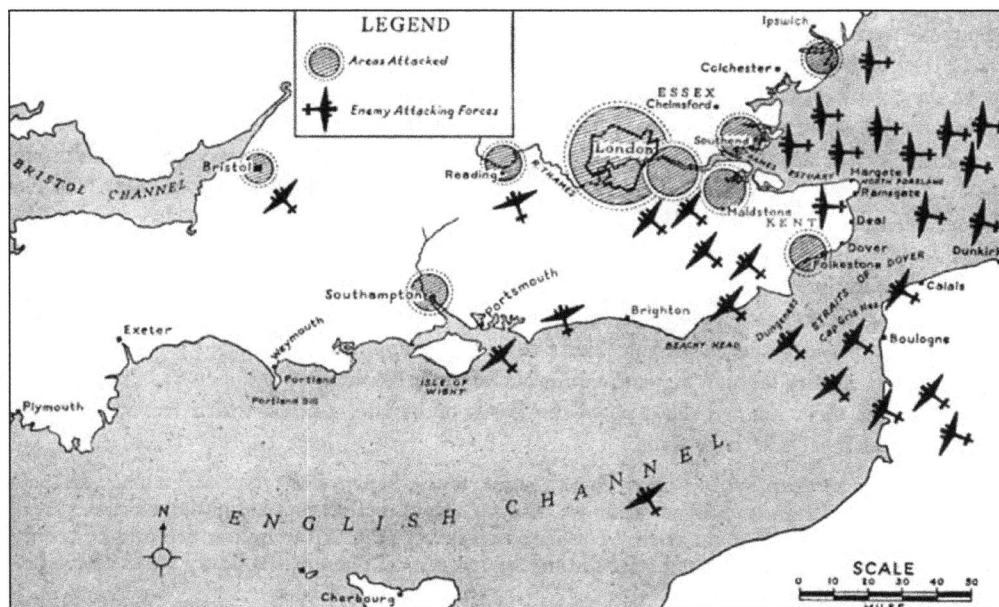

Battle of Britain Phase III: 7-27 September 1940. The day and night bombing offensive against London. NZTEC

APPENDICES

Appendix I

Boulton Paul Defiant MK.I

Specification

Powerplant: 1 Rolls Royce Merlin III 12-cylinder liquid cooled piston engine rated at 1,030 hp.
Span: 39 ft 4.in (11.99 m)
Length: 35 ft 4-in (10.77 m)
Weight: 8,218 lb (loaded)
Speed: 304 mph (490 km/h) at 17,000 ft (5,181 m)
Armament: 4 x 0.303 in Browning machine guns in an electrically operated dorsal turret behind the pilot
Crew: 2; pilot and air gunner

Appendix II

Operators of the Defiant MK.I in the day fighter role

No.264 (Madras Presidency) Squadron
No.141 Squadron

Note: Both Squadrons switched to primarily to the Night Fighter role in September 1940. No.307 (Polish) and 151 Squadrons were equipped with Defiant for the Night Fighter role by the end of 1940.

Appendix III

Operational Stations for 264 Squadron May-August 1940

RAF Duxford May 1940 (flew operations from Manston)
RAF Fowlmere early July 1940
RAF Kirton-in-Lindsey late July 1940 (Squadron went to Duxford briefly then to Kirton on 23 July)
RAF Hornchurch 22 August 1940
RAF Rochford 27 August 1940
RAF Kirton-in-Lindsey Late August 1940

Appendix IV

Me.109E

The standard single-seat fighter of the Luftwaffe during the hectic air battles of 1940 was the Messerschmitt Me.109E. A low wing monoplane, the aircraft was superior in some respects to the Hurricane and Spitfire and inferior in others. Armament was a mixture of machine guns and cannon. As with the Hurricane and Spitfire, the Me.109E had an overall superior performance to the Defiant I.

The following comes from the conclusion of a document on comparative trials between the Me.109 and a Hurricane I conducted in May 1940.

"The M.E.109 is faster than the Hurricane by some 30 to 40 miles an hour on the straight and level. It can out-climb and initially out-dive the Hurricane. On the other hand it has not the maneuverability of the Hurricane, which can turn inside without difficulty. After this clear-cut demonstration of superior maneuverability there is no doubt in my mind that provided Hurricanes are not surprised by 109's, that the odds are not more than two to one, and the pilots use their heads, the balance will always be in favour of our aircraft, one the 109's have committed themselves to combat."

Appendix V

Serviceable Defiants in Fighter Command during the three main phases of the Battle of Britain 10 July – 31 October 1940. Note: No definitive figures are available for 10-17 July

17 July:	20	17 August:	28
18 July:	23	18 August:	27
19 July:	22	19 August:	27
20 July:	11	20 August:	22
21 July:	21	21 August:	25
22 July:	22	22 August:	26
23 July:	12	23 August:	26
24 July:	15	24 August:	23
25 July:	25	25 August:	18
26 July:	26	26 August:	18
27 July:	24	27 August:	18
28 July:	26	28 August:	23
29 July:	20	29 August:	18
30 July:	23	30 August:	14
31 July:	25	31 August:	13
1 August:	21	1 September:	24
2 August:	22	2 September:	21
3 August:	24	3 September:	25
4 August:	21	4 September:	21
5 August:	26	5 September:	25
6 August:	23	6 September:	29
7 August:	24	7 September:	20
8 August:	20	8 September:	23
9 August:	23	9 September:	22
10 August:	22	10 September:	21
11 August:	24	11 September:	21
12 August:	24	12 September:	21
13 August:	26	13 September:	18
14 August:	25	14 September:	16
15 August:	25	15 September:	24
16 August:	24	16 September:	19

17 September:	23		26 October:	10
18 September:	25		27 October:	15
19 September:	21		28 October:	18
20 September:	21		29 October:	13
21 September:	27		30 October:	11
22 September:	20		31 October:	10
23 September:	18			
24 September:	19			
25 September:	19			
26 September:	15			
27 September:	19			
28 September:	19			
29 September:	16			
30 September:	13			
1 October:	17			
2 October:	19			
3 October:	12			
4 October:	20			
5 October:	15			
6 October:	18			
7 October:	9			
8 October:	14			
9 October:	17			
10 October:	14			
11 October:	18			
12 October:	16			
13 October:	13			
14 October:	19			
15 October:	18			
16 October:	17			
17 October:	17			
18 October:	16			
19 October:	22			
20 October:	20			
21 October:	13			
22 October:	19			
23 October:	26			
24 October:	12			
25 October:	12			

GLOSSARY

AA	Anti Aircraft
AFDU	Air Fighting Development Unit
AG	Air Gunner
A.W.	Armstrong Whitworth
AVM	Air Vice Marshal
BEF	British Expeditionary Force
CO	Commanding Officer
Cpl	Corporal
DFM	Distinguished Flying Medal
Do	Dornier
DSO	Distinguished Service Order
E	East
E/A	Enemy Aircraft
F	Fighter
Ft	feet
He	Heinkel
I	1
II	2
Ju	Junkers
LAC	Leading Aircraftsman
M	Meter
Me	Mess
MU	Maintenance Unit
No	Number
OC	Officer Commanding
P/O	Pilot Officer
RAF	Royal Air Force
SE	South East
Sgt	Sergeant
S/Ldr	Squadron Leader
W	West

BIBLIOGRAPHY

No.264 Squadron Operations Record Book Form 540 October 1939 – September 1940

No.264 Squadron Operations Record Book Form 541 May – September 1940

No.141 Squadron Operations Record Book Form 540 1939-September 1940

No.141 Squadron Operations Record Book Form 541 May-September 1940

No.264 Squadron Intelligence Combat Reports 24 August 1940

No.264 Squadron Intelligence Combat Reports 26 August 1940

Fighter Command 12 Group Intelligence Combat Report 24 May 1940

Fighter Command 11 Group Intelligence Combat Report 24 May 1940

Fighter Command 11 Group Intelligence Combat Reports 25 May 1940

Fighter Command 12 Group Intelligence Combat Reports 28 May 1940

No.141 Squadron Personal Combat Reports 19 July 1940

No.264 Squadron Personal Combat Reports May 1940

No.264 Squadron Personal Combat Reports August 1940

History of the Second World War, United Kingdom Military Series, The Defence of the United Kingdom, 1957 HMSO

History of the Second World War, The RAF 1939-45 Volume I, 1953 HMSO

The German Air Force in France and the Low Countries 1940, Volume I-III

Report on Sweep over The Hague from S/Ldr. Leigh, Blue Section Leader of No.66 Squadron

No.66 Squadron Operations Record Book Form 540 May 1940

No.66 Squadron Operations Record Book Form 541 May 1940

In addition hundreds of miscellaneous pages of documents; flight test, development, operational, command and political were consulted.

ABOUT THE AUTHOR

Hugh, a historian and author, has published in excess of thirty books; non-fiction and fiction, writing under his own name as well as utilising two different Pseudonyms. He has also written for several international magazines, while his work has been used as reference for many other projects ranging from the aviation industry, international news corporations, film media to encyclopedias and the computer gaming industry. He currently resides in his native Scotland

Other titles by the Author include

British Battlecruisers of World War 1 – Operational Log, July 1914-June 1915
Hurricane IIB Combat Log – 151 Wing RAF North Russia 1941
RAF Meteor Jet Fighters in World War II, An Operational Log
Typhoon IA/B Combat Log - Operation Jubilee August 1942
Eurofighter Typhoon – Storm over Europe
Tornado F.2/F.3 Air Defence Variant
Boeing X-36 – Tailless Agility Flight Research Aircraft
X-32 – The Boeing Joint Strike Fighter
X-35 – Progenitor to the F-35 Lightning II
X-45 Uninhabited Combat Air Vehicle
F-84 Thunderjet – Republic Thunder
USAF Jet Powered Fighters – XP-59-XF-85
XF-92 – Convairs Arrow
The Battle Cruiser Fleet at Jutland
Light Battlecruisers and the 2nd Battle of Heligoland Bight
Saab Gripen, The Nordic Myth
American Teens
Dassault Rafale – The Gallic Squall
Boeing F/A-18E/F Super Hornet

www.ingramcontent.com/pod-product-compliance
Lightning Source LLC
Chambersburg PA
CBHW081420090426
42738CB00017B/3426